• Bartholo...

HANDY ROA...

SCOTLAND

C000145895

KEY TO MAP PAGES

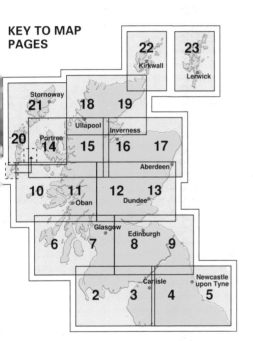

Contents

2-23	Road Maps at 9 miles to 1 inch
24-25	Urban Area Maps at 4 miles to 1 inch
24	Aberdeen, Dundee
25	Edinburgh, Glasgow
26-30	**Index to place names**
31-72	**City Plans at 4 inches to 1 mile**
31	Key to City Plan Pages
32-35	Aberdeen
36-37	Index to Aberdeen
38-39	Dundee
40-41	Index to Dundee
42-49	Edinburgh
50-55	Index to Edinburgh
56-65	Glasgow
66-72	Index to Glasgow

© Bartholomew 1993
First published 1992
New edition 1993
Published by Bartholomew, a Division of HarperCollins Publishers

Bartholomew, Duncan Street, Edinburgh EH9 1TA

Printed and bound in Great Britain by Bartholomew, The Edinburgh Press

E/B5981

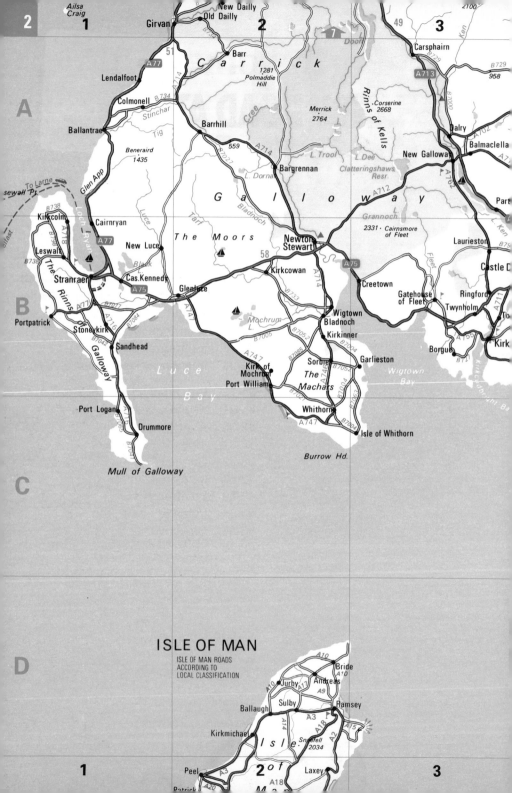

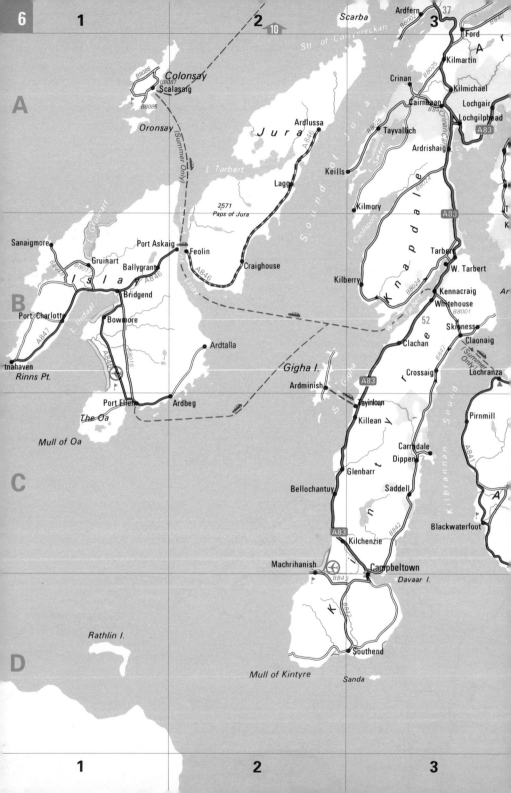

A

B

C

D

Map labels:

Scarba

Ardfern
B8007
37
B840
Ford
Kilmartin
Crinan
B8025
Kilmichael
Cairnbaan
Lochgair
B841
Lochgilphead
A83

Colonsay
B8086
B8087
Scalasaig
B8085

Oronsay

(Summer Only)

Jura
Ardlussa
A846
Tayvallich
B8025

L Tarbert
Keills
Ardrishaig
Lagg
B8024

2571
Paps of Jura
Kilmory
Knapdale
A83

Sanaigmore
Port Askaig
Tarbert
B8001
Gruinart
Feolin
W. Tarbert
Ballygrant
A846
Craighouse
Kennacraig
Islay
A846
Kilberry
Whitehouse
B8001
Bridgend
Skipness
Claonaig
Port Charlotte
Bowmore
B8024
Clachan
B842
(Summer Only)
A847
L Indaal
B8016
Ardtalla
Gigha I.
Crossaig
Lochranza
A846
Rinns Pt.
Ardminish
A83
Tayinloan
S of Gigha

tnahaven
Port Ellen
Ardbeg
Killean
Pirnmill
A841
The Oa
Carradale
Dippen
Mull of Oa
Glenbarr
Saddell

Bellochantuy
B842
Blackwaterfoot
A83
Kilchenzie
Machrihanish
Campbeltown
B843
Davaar I.
K
B842

Rathlin I.
Southend
Mull of Kintyre
Sanda

L Gruinart

Sound of Jura

L Sween

L Caolisport

W Loch Tarbert

Kilbrannan Sound

52

10

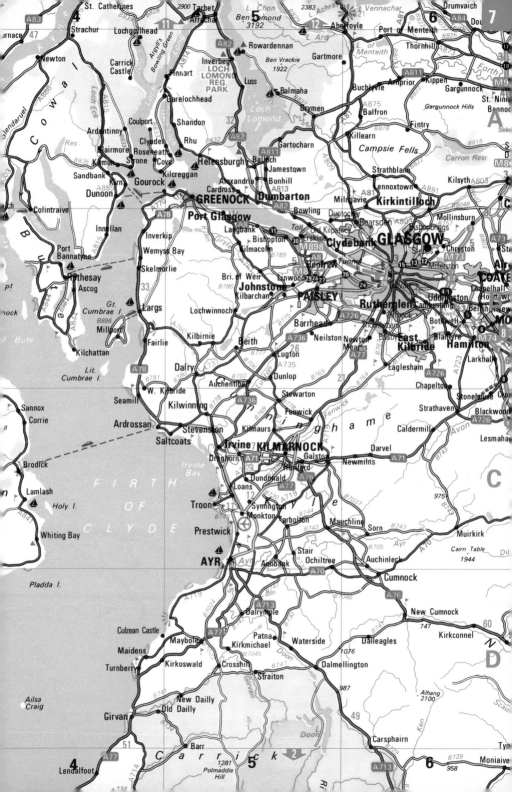

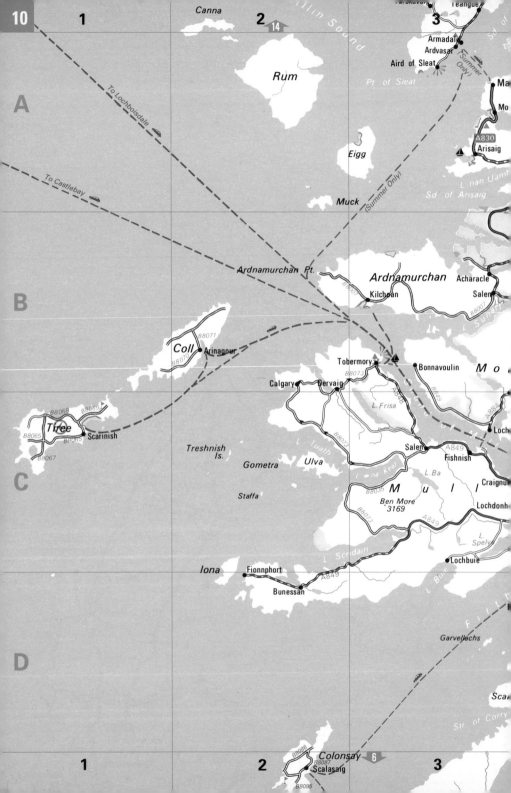

Canna

1

2 14

3

Teangue

Rum

Armadale
Ardvasar
Aird of Sleat

Pt of Sleat

Ma

Mo

A

To Lochboisdale

Eigg

A830 Arisaig

To Castlebay

Muck

L nan Uamh

Sd of Arisaig

(Summer Only)

Ardnamurchan Pt.

Ardnamurchan Acharacle

B8071 Kilchoan Salen

L Sunar

B

B8071

Coll B8070 Arinagour

Tobermory

Bonnavoulin *Mo*

B8073 A848

B8068 B8069

B8065 B8065

Tiree Scarinish

L.Frisa

A868

Calgary Dervaig

B8067

Treshnish Is.

Gometra *Ulva*

B8073

L Tuath

Salen

A849

Fishnish

Loch

C

Staffa

B8035

L na Keal

L.Ba

Craignu

M u l l

B8072

Ben More
3169

A849

Lochdonh

L. Spelv

Iona Fionnphort

L Scridain

Lochbuie

Bunessan A849

L Buie

D

Garvellachs

Fillin

Sca

Str of Corry

1

2

B8086 *Colonsay* 6

B8087 Scalasaig

3

B8085

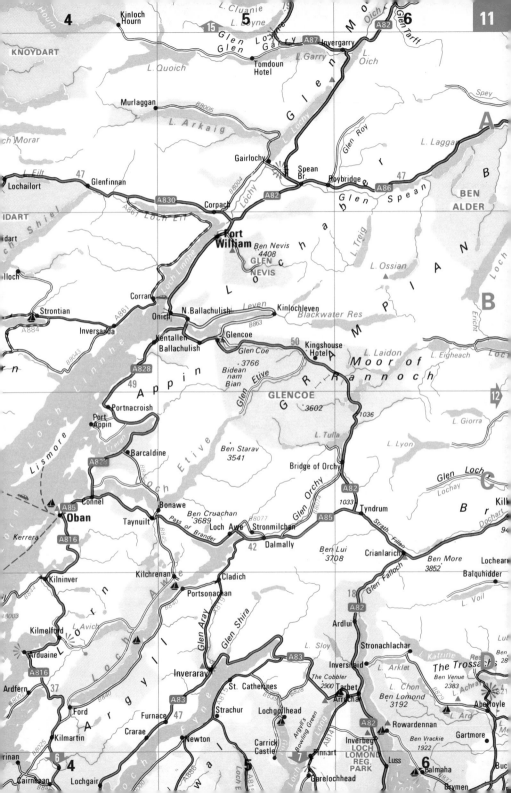

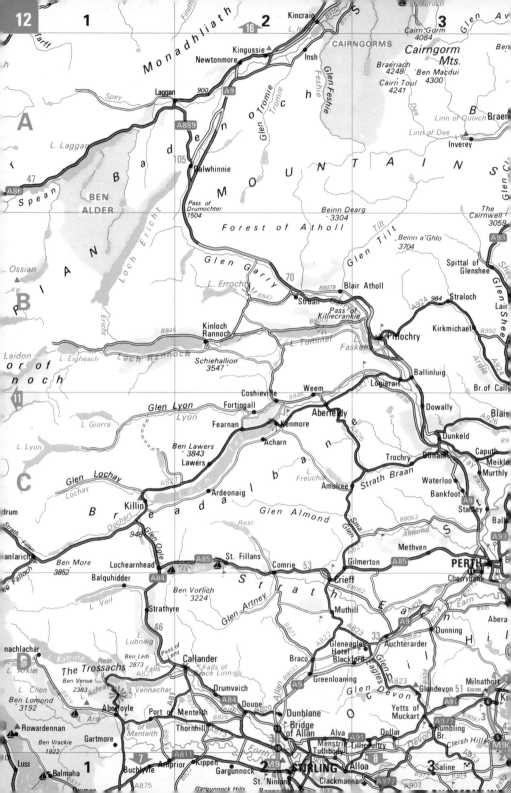

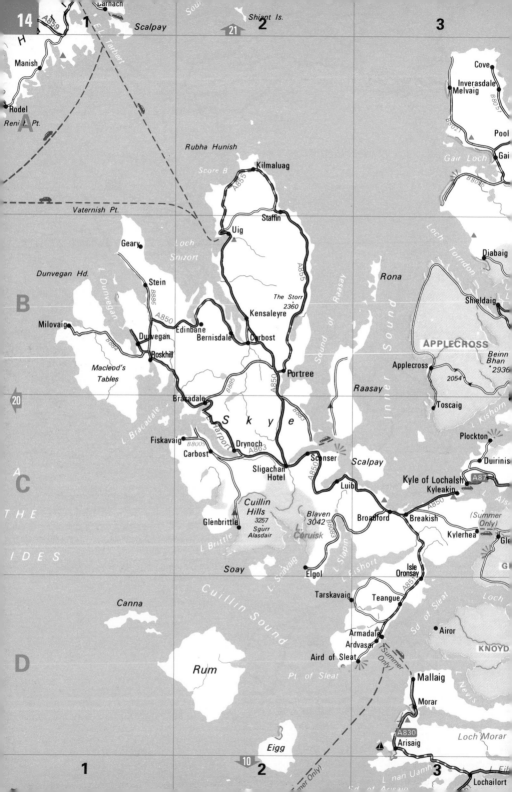

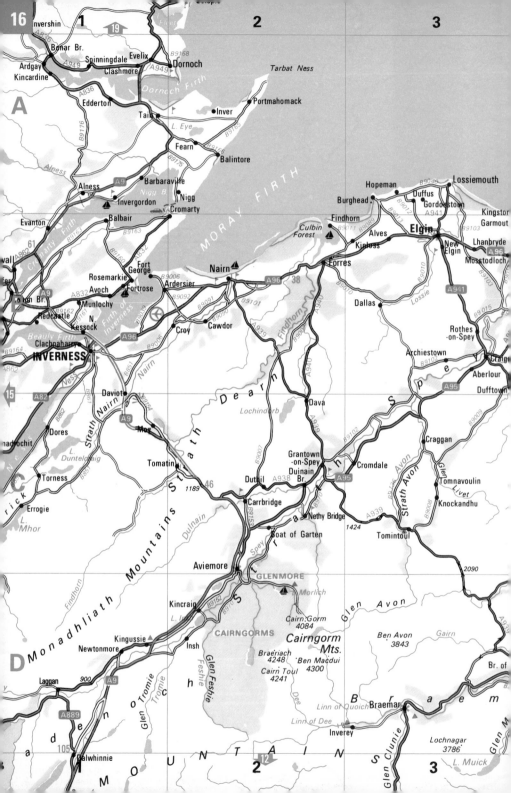

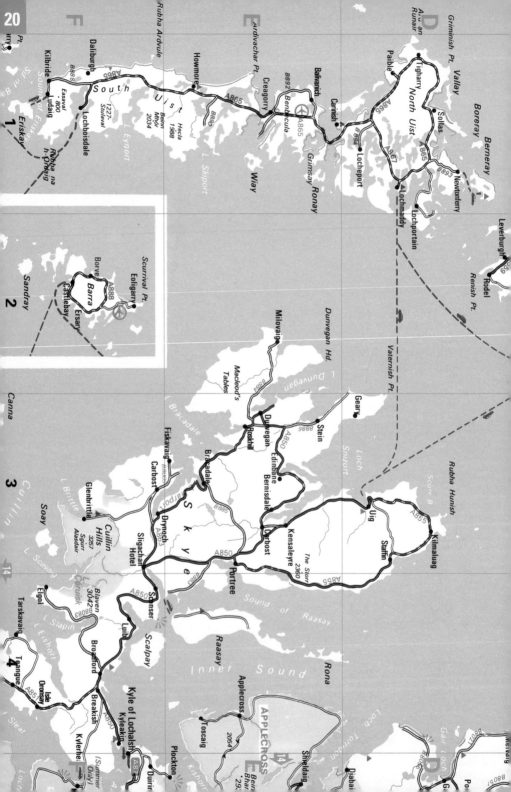

F **E** **D**

Pt
orry

Rubha Ardvule

Griminish Pt. Vallay

A' an
Runair

Grimsay

1

Kilbride
Dalliburgh
Howmore
Creagorry
Balivanich
Carinish
Pable
Tigharry
Sollas
Newtonferry
Boreray
Berneray

B888
Ludaig
Eriskay
Lochboisdale
Esaval
· 800
1227·
Stuleval
Hecla
1988
Benn
Mhor
2034
Benbecula
A865
A865
Lochportain
B892
B894
A894
A865
A865
A867
865
B893
Leverburgh
Rodel

South Uist

North Uist

Sd. of Barra

Sound of Eriskay

Rubha na
h-Ordaig

L. Skiport

Eynort

Wiay

L. Eynort

Grimsay Ronay

Lochmaddy

Vallay

Vaternish Pt.

Renish Pt.

2

Sandray

Borve
Castlebay
Ersary
Eoligarry
Scurrival Pt.
Barra
A888

Dunvegan Hd.

Milovaig

Macleod's
Tables

Geary

Stein

9888

L. Dunvegan

A850

Rubha Hunish

3

Canna

Cuillin

Soay

L. Brittle

Fiskavaig
Carbost
Glenbrittle
Drynoch
Cuillin
Hills
3257
Sgurr
Alasdair
Sligachan
Hotel

L. Bracadale

Bracadale

Dunvegan
Roskhill
Edinbane
Bernisdale

A863
A850
B885
B885

S K Y E

A850

Portree

Lochbost
Kensaleyre
Uig
Staffin
Kilmaluag
A855
A855

The Storr
2360

Rubha Hunish

Loch Snizort

Sgurr B

4

Eigol
Tarskavaig
Tpangue
A881
Isle
Oronsay
Breakish
Kylerhe
Kyleakin
Kyle of Lochalsh
Broadford
Luib
Sconser
Scalpay
Blaven
3042
L. Slapin
L. Eishort
B8083
A850
A852
A851
A87

L. Scavaig

Raasay

Rona

Sound of Raasay

Inner Sound

Applecross
2054
Toscaig
Plockton
Duirir

APPLECROSS

Sheldaig
Beinn
Bhan
· 29

Loch Torridon

Loch Kishorn

(Summer
Only)

Gair Loch Ba

B8057

Po

Diabai

14
E
D

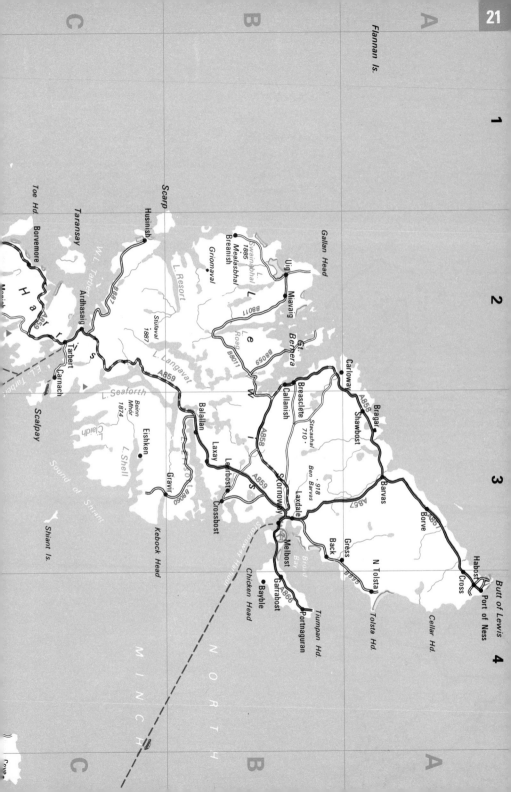

A   B   C

1   2   3   4

Flannan Is.

Scarp
Husinish
Taransay
Toe Hd.
Bornemore
Hav
Ardhasaig
Tarbert
Carnach
Scalpay
Shiant Is.

W.L.Tarbert
B887
A859

Uig
Miavaig
Gallan Head
L. Roag
B8011
B8059
Gt. Bernera

Swainbhal 1885
L. Langavat
L. Resort
Mealasbhal
Breanish
Griomaval
Stulaval 1887

L. Seaforth
Beinn Mhòr 1874
Eishken
L. Claidh
L. Shell
Gravir
Crossbost
Kebock Head

Balallan
Laxay
Leurbost
A859

Carloway
Breasclete
Callanish
Shawbost
Bragar
A858
Barvas
A857
Borve
A857
A858

Stacashal 710
Ben Barvas 918

Stornoway
Laxdale
A859

Gress
Back
N Tolsta
A857
B895
Tolsta Hd.

Cross
Habbost
Butt of Lewis
Port of Ness
Cellar Hd.

Melbost
Broad Bay
Chicken Head
Garrabost
Bayble
Portnaguran
Tiumpan Hd.
A866

MINCH
NORTH
Sound of Shiant

Cove

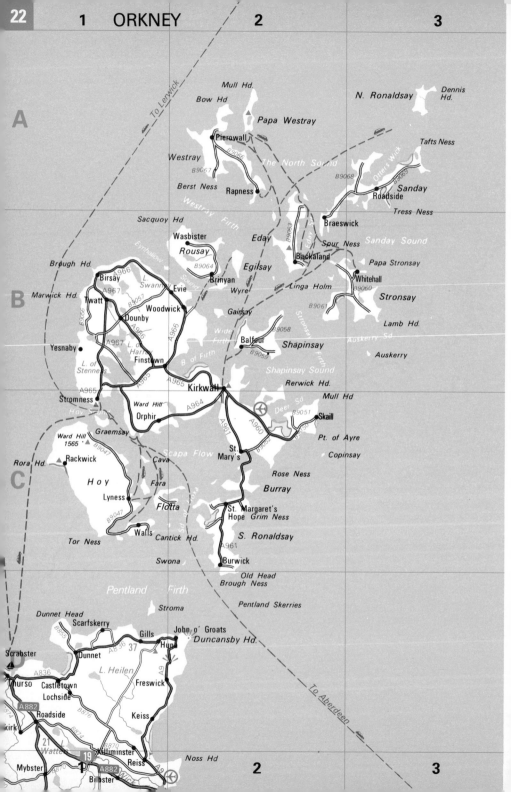

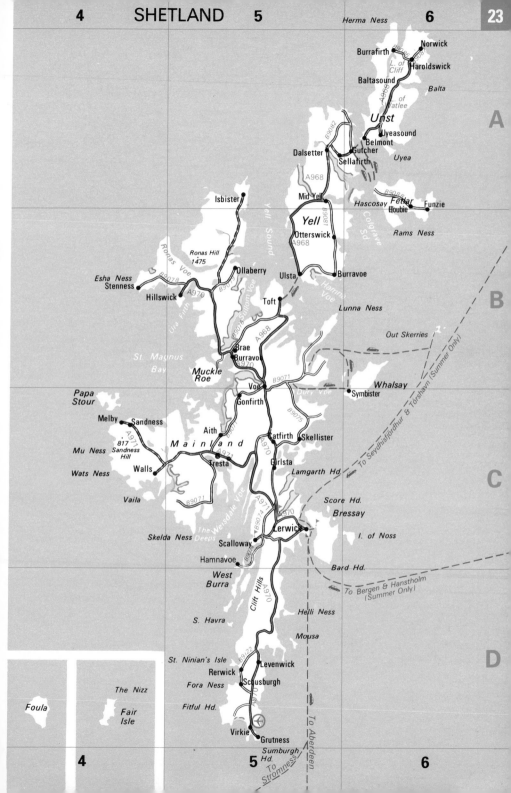

Herma Ness

Norwick
Burrafirth
L. of Cliff
Haroldswick
Baltasound
Balta
of atlee
Unst

A

Uyeasound
Belmont
Dalsetter
Gutcher
Uyea
Sellafirth

A968

Isbister

Mid Yell
Fetlar
Hascosay
Funzie
Houbie
Yell Sound

Yell

Ronas Hill
1475
Ollaberry
Otterswick
A968
Rams Ness

Esha Ness
Stenness
Ulsta
Burravoe

B

Hillswick
Ura Firth
Toft
Lunna Ness

Out Skerries

St. Magnus
Bay
Brae
Burravoe
A970
Voe
Whalsay

Muckle
Roe
Symbister

To Seydhisfjördhur & Tórshavn (Summer Only)

Papa
Stour
Gonfirth

Melby
Sandness
Aith
Catfirth
Skellister

Mu Ness
817
Sandness
Hill
Mainland
Aith
Girlsta

C

Wats Ness
Walls
Tresta
Lamgarth Hd.

Vaila
Score Hd.

Bressay

The
Deeps
Skelda Ness
Lerwick
I. of Noss

Scalloway
Bard Hd.

Hamnavoe
To Bergen & Hanstholm
(Summer Only)

**West
Burra**
Clift Hills

S. Havra
Helli Ness

Mousa

St. Ninian's Isle
Levenwick

D

Rerwick
Fora Ness
Scousburgh

Fitful Hd.

Virkie
Grutness
Sumburgh
Hd.
To Aberdeen
To
Stromness

The Nizz

Foula

Fair
Isle

4   5   6

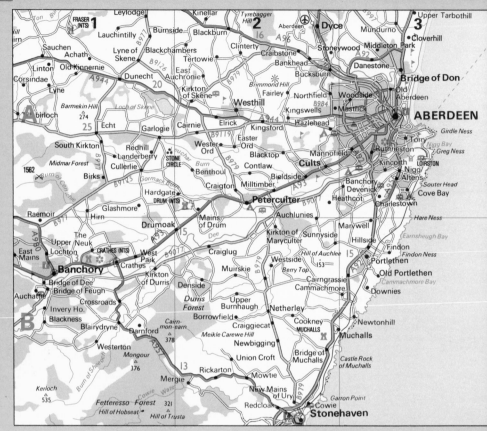

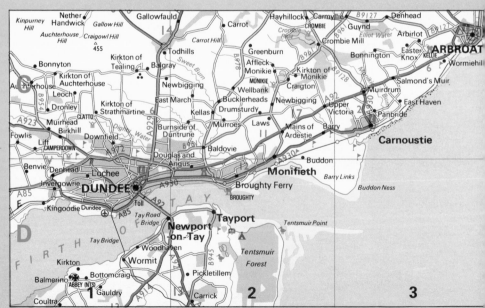

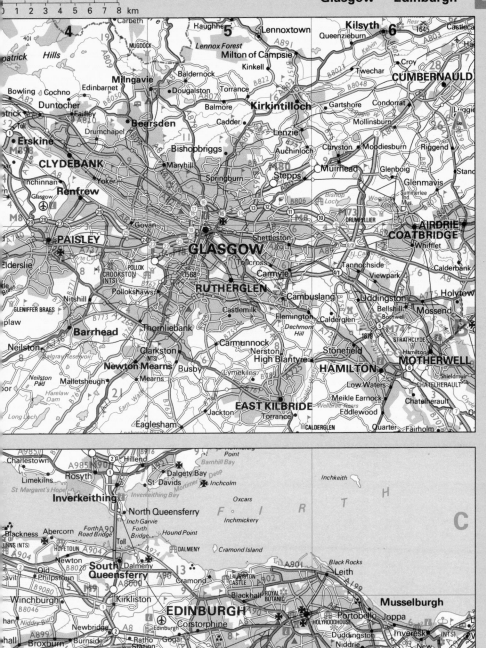

Abbreviations

Bor.	Borders	D.&G.	Dumfries & Galloway	Nor.	Northumberland	Str.	Strathclyde
Cen.	Central	Grm.	Grampian	N.Y.	North Yorkshire	Tay.	Tayside
Cum.	Cumbria	Hgh.	Highland	Ork.	Orkney	W.I.	Western Isles
		Ltn.	Lothian	She.	Shetland		

A

9 B4 Abbey St. Bathans
3 B5 Abbey Town
12 D3 Aberargie
17 B4 Aberchirder
25 C4 Abercorn
8 A2 Aberdour
12 C2 Aberfeldy
12 D1 Aberfoyle
8 A3 Aberlady
16 B3 Aberlour
13 D4 Abernethy
8 C1 Abington
13 A5 Aboyne
10 B3 Acharacle
12 C2 Acharn
24 A1 Achath
19 B5 Achavanich
18 C1 Achiltibuie
15 B4 Achintee
15 B5 Achnasheen
9 D6 Acklington
24 C2 Affleck
5 D4 Ainderby Steeple
10 A3 Aird of Sleat
25 A6 Airdrie
8 A1 Airth
23 C5 Aith
4 D3 Aldbrough
7 A5 Alexandria
17 C4 Alford
4 B2 Allendale Town
4 B2 Allenheads
8 A1 Alloa
3 B5 Allonby
16 A1 Alness
9 D6 Alnmouth
9 D6 Alnwick
4 B2 Alston
18 C3 Altassmore
24 A3 Altens
18 B3 Altnaharra
8 A1 Alva
16 B3 Alvin
9 D5 Alwinton
13 C4 Alyth
9 D6 Amble
3 D6 Ambleside
12 C2 Amulree
9 C5 Ancroft
3 B5 Annan
7 C5 Annbank
13 D5 Anstruther
4 C1 Appleby
14 B3 Applecross
24 C3 Arbirlot
24 C3 Arbroath
16 B3 Archiestown
6 C1 Ardbeg
15 A5 Ardcharnich
7 A4 Ardentinny
12 C2 Ardeonaig
16 B1 Ardersier
11 D4 Ardfern
15 A6 Ardgay
21 C2 Ardhasaig
11 D6 Ardlui
6 A2 Ardlussa
18 C2 Ardmair
6 B2 Ardminish
6 A3 Ardrishaig
7 C4 Ardrossan

6 B2 Ardtalla
11 D4 Arduaine
10 A3 Ardvasar
17 C4 Ardwell
10 B2 Arinagour
10 A3 Arisaig
8 B1 Armadale Ltn.
10 A3 Armadale Hgh.
4 B1 Armathwaite
14 D3 Arnisdale
7 A6 Arnprior
11 D6 Arrochar
7 B4 Ascog
5 A4 Ashington
8 C3 Ashkirk
4 D2 Askrigg
3 B5 Aspatria
24 B1 Auchattie
3 B4 Auchencairn
7 B5 Auchentiber
13 A6 Auchinblae
17 B4 Auchindown
7 C6 Auchinleck
25 A5 Auchinloch
24 A2 Auchlunies
12 D3 Auchterarder
24 C1 Auchterhouse
13 D4 Auchtermuchty
15 A4 Aultbea
16 C2 Aviemore
16 B1 Avoch
7 C5 Ayr
9 B5 Ayton

B

21 B3 Back
22 B2 Backaland
18 B2 Badcall
18 D1 Badluachrach
21 B3 Balallan
16 B1 Balbair
12 C3 Balbeggie
25 A5 Baldernock
24 C2 Baldovie
25 D5 Balerno
22 B2 Balfour
7 A6 Balfron
24 C1 Balgray
16 A2 Balintore
20 E1 Balivanich
11 B5 Ballachulish
2 A1 Ballantrae
13 A4 Ballater
12 B3 Ballinluig
7 A5 Balloch
6 B1 Ballygrant
2 A3 Balmaclellan
7 A5 Balmaha
24 D1 Balmerino
25 A5 Balmore
13 D4 Balmullo
12 D1 Balquhidder
9 C6 Bamburgh
4 C1 Bampton
24 B1 Banchory
24 A3 Banchory-Devenick
17 B5 Banff
3 B5 Bankend
12 C3 Bankfoot
24 A2 Bankhead
8 A1 Bannockburn
16 A1 Barbaraville

11 C4 Barcaldine
4 B2 Bardon Mill
2 A2 Bargrennan
4 C3 Barnard Castle
2 A2 Barr
25 B4 Barrhead
2 A2 Barrhill
24 C2 Barry
4 D3 Barton
21 A3 Barvas
8 B2 Bathgate
21 B4 Bayble
9 C6 Beadnell
9 C5 Beal
25 A4 Bearsden
8 D2 Beattock
15 B6 Beauly
3 B5 Beckfoot
5 A4 Bedlington
7 B5 Beith
9 C6 Belford
4 A2 Bellingham
6 C2 Bellochantuy
25 B6 Bellshill
23 A6 Belmont
4 A3 Belsay
24 A2 Benthoul
24 D1 Benvie
14 B2 Bernisdale
19 C5 Berriedale
17 B4 Berryhillock
9 B5 Berwick-upon-Tweed
19 A4 Bettyhill
24 A2 Bieldside
8 C2 Biggar
19 A6 Bilbster
9 C4 Birgham
24 C1 Birkhill
24 A1 Birks
12 C3 Birnam
22 B1 Birsay
4 C2 Bishop Auckland
25 A5 Bishopbriggs
7 B5 Bishopton Str.
8 B2 Blackburn Ltn.
24 A2 Blackburn Grm.
24 A2 Blackchambers
12 D3 Blackford
25 D5 Blackhall
24 B1 Blackness
25 C4 Blackness
24 A2 Blacktop
6 C3 Blackwaterfoot
8 C1 Blackwood
2 B2 Bladnoch
12 B2 Blair Atholl
24 B1 Blairdryne
13 C4 Blairgowrie
7 A4 Blairmore
4 B2 Blanchland
5 A4 Blyth
8 C2 Blyth Bridge
8 S2 Bo'ness
16 C2 Boat of Garten
16 A1 Bonar Bridge
11 C4 Bonawe
9 D4 Bonchester Bridge
7 A5 Bonhill
10 B3 Bonnavoulin
25 D6 Bonnyrigg
24 C1 Bonnyton

3 D5 Bootle
3 A5 Boreland
2 B3 Borgue D.&G.
19 B5 Borgue Hgh.
3 C5 Borrowdale
24 B2 Borrowfield
20 F2 Borve W.I.
21 A3 Borve W.I.
21 C2 Borvemore
3 C5 Bothel
24 D1 Bottomcraig
4 D3 Bowes
3 D6 Bowland Bridge
25 A4 Bowling
6 B1 Bowmore
3 D6 Bowness
14 C2 Bracadale
12 D2 Braco
23 B5 Brae
12 A3 Braemar
22 A2 Braeswick
21 A3 Bragar
4 B1 Brampton
4 C3 Brancepeth
4 C3 Brandon
14 C3 Breakish
21 B2 Breanish
21 B2 Breasclete
13 B5 Brechin
6 B1 Bridgend Str.
12 C3 Bridgend Tay.
25 C4 Bridgend Lth.
17 C4 Bridge of Alford
8 A1 Bridge of Allan
12 B3 Bridge of Cally
24 B1 Bridge of Dee
24 A3 Bridge of Don
12 D3 Bridge of Earn
24 B1 Bridge of Feugh
13 A4 Bridge of Gairn
24 B2 Bridge of Muchalls
11 C6 Bridge of Orchy
7 B5 Bridge of Weir
22 B2 Brinyan
14 C3 Broadford
7 C4 Brodick
19 C4 Brora
5 C5 Brotton
4 C2 Brough
5 D5 Broughton N.Y.
8 C2 Broughton Str.
24 D2 Broughty Ferry
25 D4 Broxburn
19 B6 Bruan
7 A6 Buchlyvie
8 A2 Buckhaven
17 A4 Buckie
24 C2 Bucklerheads
24 A2 Buckpool
24 C2 Buddon
10 D2 Bunessan
16 A3 Burghead
17 B6 Burnhaven
5 D6 Burniston
9 B5 Burnmouth
24 A1 Burnside Grm.
25 D4 Burnside Ltn.
24 C2 Burnside of Duntrune
8 A2 Burntisland
23 A6 Burrafirth
23 B5 Burravoe She.
23 B5 Burravoe She.

13 C4 Burrelton
22 C2 Burwick
25 B5 Busby
3 C5 Buttermere
9 D4 Byreness

C

25 A5 Cadder
6 A3 Cairnbaan
8 S2 Cairneyhill
24 B3 Cairngrassie
24 A2 Cairnie
2 B1 Cairnryan
3 C6 Caldbeck
25 B6 Calderbank
3 D5 Calder Bridge
8 B1 Caldercruix
25 B6 Calderglen
7 C6 Caldermill
4 C3 Caldwell
10 B2 Calgary
12 D2 Callander
21 B2 Callanish
3 B6 Calthwaite
25 B5 Cambuslang
8 A1 Camelon
24 B3 Cammachmore
6 C3 Campbeltown
9 D4 Camptown
15 C5 Cannich
3 A6 Canonbie
8 D2 Capplegill
12 C3 Caputh
25 A4 Carbeth
14 C2 Carbost Hgh.
14 B2 Carbost Hgh.
7 A5 Cardross
9 C5 Carham
20 E1 Carinish
3 B6 Carlisle
8 B2 Carlops
21 B2 Carloway
8 B1 Carluke
25 B5 Carmunnock
25 B4 Carmyle
24 C3 Carmyllie
21 C2 Carnach
24 C3 Carnoustie
8 B2 Carnwath
6 C3 Carradale
16 C2 Carrbridge
24 D2 Carrick
7 A4 Carrick Castle
8 D1 Carronbridge
24 C2 Carrot
2 A3 Carsphairn
8 C1 Carstairs
9 D4 Carter Bar
20 F2 Castlebay
4 B1 Castle Carrock
3 B4 Castle Douglas
19 A5 Castledown
2 B1 Castle Kennedy
25 B5 Castlemilk
4 B3 Castleside
4 A1 Castleton Bor.
5 D5 Castleton N.Y.
23 C5 Catfirth
4 D3 Catterick
4 D3 Catterick Bridge
16 B2 Cawdor
13 D4 Ceres

7	B6	Chapelton
4	A3	Charlestown *Grm.*
5	C4	Charlestown *Fife*
5	B6	Chatelherault
9	C5	Chatton
2	C3	Cherrybank
9	C5	Chillingham
9	B5	Chirnside
5	A6	Chryston
6	B3	Clachan
8	A1	Clackmannan
6	B1	Clacknaharry
4	D5	Cladich
9	C3	Claggan
6	B3	Claonaig
3	A5	Clarencefield
6	A1	Clashmore
3	B1	Clashnessie
3	D4	Cleator
4	A2	Clinterty
7	B6	Clola
3	A4	Closeburn
3	D6	Cloughton
4	B4	Clova
8	C3	Clovenfords
4	A3	Cloverhill
5	D4	Cluanie Bridge
5	A4	Clydebank
4	A4	Clynder
5	B6	Coatbridge
5	A4	Cochno
3	B4	Cockburnspath
3	A3	Cockenzie
4	C5	Cockermouth
4	B5	Coldingham
4	C5	Coldstream
4	D5	Colinsburgh
4	D5	Colinton
7	A4	Colintraive
2	C6	Collieston
2	A1	Colmonell
4	C5	Colpy
2	C2	Comrie
2	A6	Condorrat
4	D6	Coniston
4	C4	Connel
6	B6	Conon Bridge
8	B3	Consett
5	B6	Contin
6	A2	Contlaw
2	B2	Cookney
4	B3	Corbridge
4	B4	Cornhill
4	C5	Cornhill on Tweed
4	A5	Corpach
4	B4	Corran
7	C4	Corrie
4	A5	Corrie Common
7	A1	Corsindale
7	A4	Corsock
4	D5	Corstorphine
2	C2	Coshieville
5	C3	Cotherstone
4	A4	Coulport
4	C2	Coulter
4	D1	Coultra
4	C4	Coupar Angus
4	A4	Cove *Str.*
4	A3	Cove *Hgh.*
4	A3	Cove Bay
4	A2	Cowdenbeath
4	B2	Cowie
4	C4	Coxhoe
4	C5	Crackaig
4	C3	Craggan
4	A2	Craibstone
4	B3	Craigellachie
4	B2	Craiggiecat
4	B2	Craighouse
4	D5	Craiglockhart

24	B2	Craiglug
25	D6	Craigmillar
10	C3	Craignure
13	B4	Craigton *Tay.*
24	A2	Craigton *Grm.*
24	C2	Craigton *Tay.*
13	D5	Crail
9	C4	Crailing
5	A4	Cramlington
25	C5	Cramond
7	A4	Crarae
24	B1	Crathes
5	D4	Crathorne
8	C1	Crawford
8	C1	Crawfordjohn
20	E1	Creagorry
2	B3	Creetown
11	C6	Crianlarich
12	C2	Crieff
17	B6	Crimond
6	A3	Crinan
3	A4	Crocketford
5	D4	Croft
10	C3	Croggan
16	B1	Cromarty
24	C2	Crombie Mill
16	C3	Cromdale
4	C3	Crook
3	C5	Crosby
4	C1	Crosby Ravensworth
21	A4	Cross
6	B3	Crossaig
21	B3	Crossbost
8	C1	Crossford
25	D6	Crossgatehall
8	A2	Crossgates
7	D5	Crosshill
2	B3	Crossmichael
24	B1	Crossroads
16	B2	Croy *Hgh.*
25	A6	Croy *Str.*
17	C6	Cruden Bay
4	C1	Culgaith
18	B1	Culkein
17	A4	Cullen
24	A1	Cullerlie
8	A2	Culross
24	A2	Cults
7	D4	Culzean Castle
25	A6	Cumbernauld
17	B5	Cuminestown
3	B5	Cummertrees
7	C6	Cumnock
4	B1	Cumrew
13	D4	Cupar
25	D5	Currie

D

13	D4	Dairsie
3	B4	Dalbeattie
25	C5	Dalgety Bay
20	F1	Daliburgh
25	D6	Dalkeith
7	D6	Dalleagles
11	C5	Dalmally
17	D5	Dalmellington
25	C4	Dalmeny
2	A3	Dalry *D.&G.*
7	B5	Dalry *Str.*
7	D5	Dalrymple
23	A5	Dalsetter
3	B6	Dalston
3	A5	Dalton
12	A2	Dalwhinnie
5	D5	Danby
25	D6	Danderhall
24	A3	Danestone
24	B1	Darnford
7	C6	Darvel

16	C2	Dava
16	B1	Daviot
24	C3	Denhead *Tay.*
24	D1	Denhead *Tay.*
9	D4	Denholm
8	A1	Denny
8	A1	Dennyloanhead
24	B2	Denside
10	B2	Dervaig
17	B4	Deskford
14	B3	Diabaig
15	B6	Dingwall
13	A5	Dinnet
6	C3	Dippen
8	A3	Dirleton
3	C4	Distington
9	C5	Doddington
8	A1	Dollar
8	B2	Dolphinton
16	C1	Dores
15	C4	Dornie
16	A1	Dornoch
3	B5	Dornock
25	A5	Dougalston
8	C1	Douglas
24	D2	Douglas and Angus
8	C1	Douglas Mill
22	B1	Dounby
12	D2	Doune
19	A5	Dounreay
12	C3	Dowally
24	C1	Downfield
4	D3	Downholme
24	B3	Downies
7	C5	Dreghorn
8	A3	Drem
3	D5	Drigg
24	C1	Dronley
18	B2	Drumbeg
25	A4	Drumchapel
8	C2	Drumelzier
2	C1	Drummore
15	C6	Drumnadrochit
24	B2	Drumoak
24	C2	Drumsturdy
12	D2	Drumvaich
7	A5	Drymen
14	C2	Drynoch
25	D6	Duddingston
9	C5	Duddo
16	B3	Dufftown
16	A3	Duffus
16	C2	Duinain Bridge
14	C3	Duirinish
7	A5	Dumbarton
3	A4	Dumfries
9	A4	Dunbar
19	B5	Dunbeath
12	D2	Dunblane
24	D1	Dundee
7	C5	Dundonald
15	A4	Dundonnell
2	B3	Dundrennan
24	A1	Dunecht
8	A2	Dunfermline
12	C3	Dunkeld
7	B5	Dunlop
19	A6	Dunnet
12	D3	Dunning
7	A4	Dunoon
9	B4	Duns
3	A4	Dunscore
8	B2	Dunsyre
25	A4	Duntocher
14	B1	Dunvegan
5	B4	Durham
8	D1	Durisdeer
18	A3	Durness
16	C2	Duthill
24	A2	Dyce

13	B4	Dykehead
8	A2	Dysart

E

25	B5	Eaglesham
9	C4	Earlston
11	D4	Easdale
5	B4	Easington *Drm.*
24	A2	East Auchronie
25	D4	East Calder
24	C3	Easter Knox
24	A2	Easter Ord
24	C3	East Haven
25	D6	Easthouses
25	B5	East Kilbride
9	A4	East Linton
24	B1	East Mains
24	C2	East March
3	B5	Eastriggs
8	B3	East Saltoun
8	A2	East Wemyss
8	B3	Ebchester
3	A5	Ecclefechan
9	C4	Eccles
25	A5	Ecclesmachan
24	A1	Echt
9	C4	Eckford
16	A1	Edderton
8	B2	Eddleston
25	B6	Eddlewood
14	B2	Edinbane
25	A4	Edinbarnet
25	D5	Edinburgh
9	D6	Edlingham
4	B3	Edmondbyers
9	C4	Ednam
13	B5	Edzell
9	C6	Eglingham
3	D4	Egremont
5	D6	Egton
21	C3	Eishkea
25	B4	Elderslie
16	B3	Elgin
14	C2	Elgol
5	A4	Ellington
17	C6	Ellon
18	C2	Elphin
24	A2	Elrick
4	A2	Elsdon
8	C2	Elsrickle
8	D1	Elvanfoot
9	C6	Embleton
20	F2	Eoligarry
18	A3	Eriboll
15	C6	Errogie
13	C4	Errol
25	A4	Erskine
25	D6	Eskbank
3	D5	Eskdale Green
9	C5	Etal
8	C3	Ettrickbridge
16	A1	Evelix
22	B1	Evie
25	B5	Eyemouth

F

25	A4	Faifley
25	B6	Fairholm
24	A2	Fairley
7	B4	Fairlie
25	D5	Fairmilehead
8	A1	Falkirk
13	D4	Falkland
4	A2	Falstone
19	A4	Farr
16	A2	Fearn
12	C2	Fearnan
9	D6	Felton

7	C5	Fenwick
6	B2	Feolin
13	B5	Fern
5	C4	Ferryhill
13	B5	Fettercairn
16	B2	Findhorn
17	A4	Findochty
24	B3	Findon
7	A4	Finnart
22	B5	Finstown
7	A6	Fintry
10	D2	Fionnphort
4	D1	Firbank
10	C3	Fishnish
14	C2	Fiskavaig
25	B5	Flemington
3	C5	Flimby
16	B3	Fochabers
9	C5	Ford *Nor.*
11	D4	Ford *Str.*
13	B5	Forfar
16	B2	Forres
19	B4	Forsinard Hotel
15	D5	Fort Augustus
16	B1	Fort George
12	C2	Fortingall
16	B1	Fortrose
11	B5	Fort William
24	C1	Fowlis
15	C6	Foyers
17	A6	Fraserburgh
16	A4	Freswick
13	B5	Friockheim
4	C3	Frosterley
23	A6	Funzie
7	A4	Furnace
17	B5	Fyvie

G

4	C3	Gainford
14	A3	Gairloch
11	A5	Gairlochy
8	C3	Galashiels
24	C2	Gallowfauld
7	C5	Galston
4	C1	Gamblesby
17	B5	Gardenstown
7	A4	Garelochhead
7	A6	Gargunnock
2	B3	Garlieston
24	A1	Garlogie
16	B3	Garmouth
21	B4	Garrabost
7	A5	Gartmore
7	A5	Gartocharn
25	A6	Gartshore
9	B4	Garvald
15	B5	Garve
2	B3	Gatehouse of Fleet
24	D1	Gauldry
9	B4	Gavinton
14	B1	Geary
25	A4	Georgetown
9	B4	Gifford
4	D3	Gilling
19	A6	Gills
12	C2	Gilmerton *Tay.*
25	D6	Gilmerton *Ltn.*
23	C5	Girlsta
7	D4	Girvan
13	C4	Glamis
24	A1	Glashmore
25	B5	Glasgow
6	C2	Glenbarr
25	A6	Glenboig
14	C2	Glenbrittle
3	A4	Glencaple
13	C4	Glencarse
11	B5	Glencoe

12 D3 Glendevon
12 D3 Gleneagles Hotel
14 C3 Glenelg
11 A4 Glenfinnan
13 B4 Glenisla
2 B2 Glenluce
25 A6 Glenmavis
3 C6 Glenridding
8 A3 Glenrothes
5 D6 Goathland
25 D5 Gogar
19 C4 Golspie
19 A4 Golval
23 C5 Gonfirth
9 C4 Gordon
8 C3 Gordon Arms
16 A3 Gordonstoun
8 B3 Gorebridge
3 D5 Gosforth
7 A4 Gourock
25 A4 Govan
16 C3 Graggan
3 C5 Grange
8 A1 Grangemouth
16 C2 Grantown-on-Spey
9 B5 Grantshouse
3 D6 Grasmere
21 B3 Gravir
4 D1 Grayrigg
5 D5 Great Ayton
4 C2 Great Musgrave
5 D4 Great Smeaton
24 C2 Greenburn
4 B1 Greenhead
9 B4 Greenlaw
12 D2 Greenloaning
7 A5 Greenock
21 B3 Gress
3 B6 Gretna
3 B6 Gretna Green
3 C6 Greystoke
4 D3 Grinton
21 B2 Griomaval
15 A4 Gruinard
6 B1 Gruinart
23 D5 Grutness
12 C3 Guildtown
5 C5 Guisborough
8 A3 Gullane
23 A6 Gutcher
24 C3 Guynd

H
21 A4 Habost
8 A3 Haddington
19 A5 Halkirk
4 B2 Haltwhistle
25 B6 Hamilton
23 C5 Hamnavoe
9 D5 Harbottle
24 A2 Hardgate
23 A6 Haroldswick
5 C4 Hart
4 A3 Hartburn
5 C4 Hartlepool
5 B4 Haswell
25 A4 Haughhead
4 D2 Hawes
8 D3 Hawick
3 D6 Hawkshead
4 B2 Haydon Bridge
24 C2 Hayhillock
24 A2 Hazlehead
24 A2 Heathcot
9 C4 Heiton
7 A5 Helensburgh
19 C5 Helmsdale
5 B4 Hetton le Hole

4 B2 Hexham
25 B5 High Blantyre
5 D6 High Hawsker
3 B6 High Hesket
25 C4 Hillend *Fife*
25 D5 Hillend *Ltn.*
24 B3 Hillside
23 B5 Hillswick
5 C5 Hinderwell
24 A1 Hirn
9 D4 Hobkirk
25 B6 Holytown
16 A3 Hopeman
23 A6 Houbie
20 E1 Howmore
9 C4 Hownam
19 A6 Huna
17 B4 Huntly
7 C5 Hurlford
5 D4 Hurworth
21 C2 Husinish
5 D4 Hutton Rudby

I
13 B5 Inchbare
25 A4 Inchinnan
18 C2 Inchnadamph
13 C4 Inchture
7 B4 Inellan
9 D5 Ingram
8 C3 Innerleithen
17 C5 Insch
12 A2 Insh
16 A2 Inver
14 B3 Inveralligin
17 A6 Inverallochy
18 C3 Inveran
11 D5 Inveraray
14 A3 Inverasdale
7 A5 Inverbeg
13 B6 Inverbervie
25 D6 Inveresk
14 A3 Inverewe
12 A3 Inverey
15 C6 Inverfarigaig
11 A6 Invergarry
16 A1 Invergordon
24 D1 Invergowrie
15 C4 Inverinate
13 B5 Inverkeilor
25 C4 Inverkeithing
7 B4 Inverkip
18 C1 Inverkirkaig
15 C6 Invermoriston
16 B1 Inverness
11 B4 Inversanda
15 C4 Invershiel
18 D3 Invershin
11 D6 Inversnaid
17 C5 Inverurie
24 B1 Invery House
3 C5 Ireby
7 C5 Irvine
23 A5 Isbister
2 C3 Isle of Whithorn
14 D3 Isle Oronsay

J
25 B5 Jackton
7 A5 Jamestown
19 B5 Janetstown
9 C4 Jedburgh
19 A6 John o'Groats
7 B5 Johnstone
25 D6 Joppa
25 D5 Juniper Green

K
25 D6 Kaimes
7 A4 Kames
6 A2 Keills
19 A6 Keiss
17 B4 Keith
4 D2 Keld
24 C2 Kellas
9 C4 Kelso
8 A2 Kelty
17 C5 Kemnay
4 D1 Kendal
12 C2 Kenmore
6 B3 Kennacraig
14 B2 Kensaleyre
11 B4 Kentallen
3 D6 Kentmere
3 C5 Keswick
13 D4 Kettlebridge
7 B5 Kilbarchan
6 B3 Kilberry
7 B5 Kilbirnie
20 F1 Kilbride
7 B4 Kilchattan
6 C2 Kilchenzie
10 B3 Kilchoan
11 D5 Kilchrenan
13 D5 Kilconquhar
7 A4 Kilcreggan
19 C4 Kildonan
6 A3 Kilfinan
6 C3 Killean
7 A6 Killearn
19 A6 Killimster
12 C1 Killin
7 B5 Kilmacolm
14 A2 Kilmalvag
13 C4 Kilmany
7 C5 Kilmarnock
6 A3 Kilmartin
7 C5 Kilmaurs
11 D4 Kilmelford
6 A3 Kilmichael
15 B6 Kilmorack
6 A3 Kilmory
7 A4 Kilmun
11 D4 Kilninver
13 D5 Kilrenny
25 A6 Kilsyth
7 C5 Kilwinning
19 B4 Kinbrace
8 A1 Kincardine *Fife*
16 A1 Kincardine *Hgh.*
13 A5 Kincardine O' Neil
24 A3 Kincorth
16 D2 Kincraig
24 A2 Kinellar
8 A3 Kinghorn
8 A2 Kinglassie
24 D1 Kingoodie
13 D5 Kingsbarns
24 A2 Kingsford
11 B5 Kingshouse Hotel
16 A3 Kingston
24 A2 Kingswells
12 A2 Kingussie
25 A5 Kinkell
20 A2 Kinlochbervie
15 B4 Kinlochewe
15 D4 Kinloch Hourn
11 B5 Kinlochleven
10 B3 Kinlochmoidart
12 B2 Kinloch Rannoch
16 B3 Kinloss
12 D3 Kinross
13 A5 Kintore
7 A6 Kippen
3 B4 Kippford
3 B6 Kirkbampton
3 B4 Kirkbean

3 B5 Kirkbride
4 D2 Kirkby Stephen
8 A2 Kirkcaldy
2 B1 Kirkcolm
7 D6 Kirkconnel
2 B2 Kirkcowan
2 B3 Kirkcudbright
8 C1 Kirkfieldbank
2 B2 Kirkinner
25 A5 Kirkintilloch
25 D4 Kirkliston
7 D5 Kirkmichael *Str.*
12 B3 Kirkmichael *Tay.*
9 C5 Kirknewton *Nor.*
25 D4 Kirknewton *Ltn.*
2 B2 Kirk of Mochrum
4 B1 Kirkoswald *Cum.*
7 D4 Kirkoswald *Str.*
24 D1 Kirkton
24 C1 Kirkton of Auchterhouse
24 B1 Kirkton of Durris
24 B2 Kirkton of Maryculter
24 C2 Kirkton of Monikie
24 A2 Kirkton of Skene
24 C1 Kirkton of Strathmartine
24 C1 Kirkton of Tealing
17 B5 Kirkton of Auchterless
17 C4 Kirktown of Clatt
22 B2 Kirkwall
7 A4 Kirn
13 B4 Kirriemuir
14 B3 Kishorn
4 B1 Knarsdale
16 C3 Knockandhu
14 C3 Kyleakin
14 C3 Kyle of Lochalsh
14 C3 Kylerhea
18 B2 Kyles
18 B2 Kylestrome

L
13 D4 Ladybank
6 A2 Lagg *Str.*
6 C3 Lagg *Str.*
12 A1 Laggan
15 A4 Laide
12 B3 Lair
18 C3 Lairg
8 C2 Lamington
7 C4 Lamlash
8 C1 Lanark
4 B3 Lanchester
24 A1 Landerberry
7 B5 Langbank
3 A6 Langholm
4 C1 Langwathby
8 A1 Larbert
13 D4 Largo
13 D5 Largo Ward
7 B4 Largs
25 B6 Larkhall
25 D6 Lasswade
19 B5 Latheron
24 A1 Lauchintilly
9 B4 Lauder
13 B5 Laurencekirk
2 B3 Lauriestone
24 C2 Laws
21 B3 Laxay
21 B3 Laxdale
18 B2 Laxford Bridge
4 C1 Lazonby
8 B2 Leadburn
8 D1 Leadhills
18 C2 Ledmore Lodge
25 C6 Leith

2 A1 Lendalfoot
25 A5 Lennoxtown
25 A5 Lenzie
24 C1 Leoch
23 C5 Lerwick
9 D6 Lesbury
13 D4 Leslie
8 C1 Lesmahagow
2 B1 Leswalt
13 C5 Leuchars
21 B3 Leurbost
8 A2 Leven
25 D6 Levenhall
23 D5 Levenwick
20 D2 Leverburgh
24 A1 Leylodge
16 B3 Lhanbryde
8 C2 Libberton
25 D6 Liberton
24 C1 Liff
9 C4 Lilliesleaf
25 C4 Limekilns
13 D4 Lindores
5 C5 Lingdale
8 S2 Linlithgow
17 B4 Lintmill
24 A1 Linton
7 B5 Linwood
24 D4 Livingston
25 D6 Loanhead
7 C5 Loans
11 A4 Lochailort
10 C3 Lochaline
3 A4 Locharbriggs
11 C5 Loch Awe
20 F1 Lochboisdale
10 C3 Lochbuie
15 B4 Lochcarron
10 C3 Lochdonhead
12 C1 Lochearnhead
24 D1 Lochee
20 D1 Locheport
6 A3 Lochgair
8 A2 Lochgelly
6 A3 Lochgilphead
7 A4 Lochgoilhead
18 C2 Lochinver
3 A5 Lochmaben
20 D1 Lochmaddy
15 A4 Loch Maree Hotel
20 D1 Lochportain
6 B3 Lochranza
19 A6 Lochside
7 B5 Lochwinnoch
3 A5 Lockerbie
5 C5 Loftus
12 B3 Logierait
13 C4 Longforgan
9 B4 Longformacus
9 D6 Longframlington
25 D6 Long Hermiston
4 A3 Longhirst
4 A3 Longhorsley
9 D6 Longhoughton
17 B5 Longmanhill
8 A3 Longniddry
3 A6 Longtown
17 A3 Lossiemouth
9 C5 Lowick
25 B6 Low Waters
20 F1 Ludaig
25 A6 Luggiebank
7 B5 Lugton
14 C2 Luib
17 D4 Lumphanan
17 C4 Lumsden
7 A5 Luss
19 B6 Lybster
25 B5 Lymekilns
24 A1 Lyne

A1 Lyne of Skene
C1 Lyness
C6 Lythe

M
B5 Macduff
C2 Machrihanish
B3 Macmerry
C4 Maidens
C2 Mains of Ardestie
A2 Mains of Drum
A3 Mallaig
D5 Malleny Mills
B4 Malletsheugh
C2 Manish
A3 Mannofield
D4 Markinch
C5 Marske
B6 Marybank
A6 Maryculter
A5 Maryhill
B5 Marykirk
C5 Maryport
A5 Marywell Grm.
C5 Marywell Tay.
B3 Marywell Grm.
A2 Mastrick
C5 Mauchline
C4 Maxton
A4 Maxwelltown
D5 Maybole
B4 Mearns
C4 Meigle
B6 Meikle Earnock
C3 Meikleour
C4 Melby
A3 Mellon Charles
C1 Melmerby
B2 Mergie
C5 Methlick
C3 Methven
D2 Miavaig
D4 Mid Calder
C2 Middleton in Teesdale
A3 Middleton Park
B1 Midgeholme
A5 Mid Yell
D6 Millerhill
B4 Millport
A2 Milltimber
D3 Milnathort
A4 Milngavie
B1 Milovaig
A5 Milton of Campsie
B6 Mintlaw
A3 Mitford
D2 Moffat
A6 Mollinsburn
A4 Moniaive
D2 Monifieth
C2 Monikie
C5 Monkton
B4 Montrose
C5 Monymusk
A6 Moodiesburn
A3 Morar
C4 Morebattle
A3 Moresby
D5 Morningside
A3 Morpeth
C4 Mossat

25 B6 Mossend
8 D3 Mosspaul Hotel
16 B3 Mosstodloch
25 B6 Motherwell
3 A5 Mouswald
24 B2 Mowtie
16 C1 Moy
24 B2 Muchalls
24 C3 Muirdrum
24 C1 Muirhead Tay.
25 A6 Muirhead Str.
7 C6 Muirkirk
17 C4 Muir of Fowlis
15 B6 Muir of Ord
24 B2 Muirskie
4 D2 Muker
24 A3 Mundurno
16 B1 Munlochy
11 A4 Murlaggan
24 C2 Murroes
12 C3 Murthly
25 D6 Musselburgh
12 D2 Muthill
19 A5 Mybster

N
16 B2 Nairn
4 D2 Nateby
25 B4 Neilston
4 B2 Nenthead
9 C4 Nenthorn
24 C1 Nether Handwick
24 B2 Netherley
4 A3 Netherwitton
16 C2 Nethy Bridge
24 B1 Neuk, The
3 B4 New Abbey
17 B5 New Aberdour
8 B1 Newarthill
4 D2 Newbiggin
5 A4 Newbiggin-by-the-Sea
8 C2 Newbigging Str.
24 B2 Newbigging Grm.
24 C1 Newbigging Tay.
24 C2 Newbigging Tay.
25 D4 Newbridge
13 D4 Newburgh Fife
17 C6 Newburgh Grm.
17 B5 Newbyth
3 A6 Newcastleton
25 D6 New Craighall
7 D6 New Cumnock
7 D5 New Dailly
17 B5 New Deer
16 B3 New Elgin
2 A3 New Galloway
2 B1 New Luce
17 C5 Newmachar
8 B1 Newmains
24 B2 New Mains of Ury
7 C6 Newmilns
17 B5 New Pitsligo
24 D1 Newport-on-Tay
12 C3 New Scone
7 A4 Newton Str.
25 C4 Newton Ltn.
3 B5 Newton Arlosh
20 D1 Newtonferry
8 B3 Newtongrange
24 B3 Newtonhill
25 B4 Newton Mearns
12 A2 Newtonmore
9 D6 Newton on the Moor
2 B2 Newton Stewart
9 C4 Newtown St. Boswells
13 C4 Newtyle
25 D6 Niddrie

16 A2 Nigg Hgh.
24 A3 Nigg Grm.
25 B4 Nitshill
9 B5 Norham
5 D4 Northallerton
11 B5 North Ballachulish
9 A4 North Berwick
24 A2 Northfield
16 B1 North Kessock
25 C4 North Queensferry
9 C6 North Sunderland
21 A4 North Tolsta
23 A6 Norwick

O
25 D4 Oakbank
11 C4 Oban
19 B6 Occumster
7 C5 Ochiltree
24 A3 Old Aberdeen
25 D6 Old Craighall
7 D4 Old Dailly
17 B6 Old Deer
25 A4 Old Kilpatrick
24 A1 Old Kinnernie
17 C5 Oldmeldrum
25 C4 Old Philipstoun
24 B3 Old Portlethen
23 B5 Ollaberry
11 B5 Onich
13 A5 Orbost
8 B3 Ormiston
22 C1 Orphir
4 D1 Orton
4 A2 Otterburn
6 A3 Otter Ferry
23 B5 Otterswick
3 B5 Oulton
18 C3 Oykel Bridge
17 C5 Oyne

P
20 D1 Paible
25 B4 Paisley
3 B4 Palnackie
24 C3 Panbride
3 A4 Parkgate
2 A3 Parton
8 B3 Pathhead
7 D5 Patna
3 C6 Patterdale
8 C3 Peebles
8 B3 Pencaitland
8 B2 Penicuik
17 A5 Pennan
3 A4 Penpont
4 C1 Penrith
12 C3 Perth
24 A2 Peterculter
17 B6 Peterhead
5 B4 Peterlee
25 C4 Philipstoun
24 D2 Pickletillen
4 C3 Piercebridge
22 A2 Pierowall
6 C3 Pirnmill
12 B3 Pitlochry
13 D4 Pitscottie
19 C4 Pittentrail
13 D5 Pittenweem
8 A1 Plean
14 C3 Plockton
6 C1 Plumpton Wall
11 B4 Polloch
25 B5 Pollockshaws
8 A1 Polmont
14 A3 Poolewe
3 C6 Pooley Bridge

11 C4 Port Appin
6 B2 Port Askaig
7 B4 Port Bannatyne
3 B5 Port Carlisle
6 B1 Port Charlotte
6 C1 Port Ellen
17 A4 Portessie
7 B5 Port Glasgow
19 C5 Portgower
24 B3 Portlethen
2 C1 Port Logan
16 A2 Portmahomack
11 C4 Portnacroish
21 B4 Portnaguran
6 B1 Portnahaven
17 A4 Portnockie
25 D6 Portobello
7 A6 Port of Menteith
21 A4 Port of Ness
2 B1 Portpatrick
14 B2 Portree
19 A4 Portskerra
11 D5 Portsonachan
17 A4 Port Soy
2 B2 Port William
9 B4 Preston
8 A3 Prestonpans
7 C5 Prestwick
25 D4 Pumpherston

Q
25 B6 Quarter
25 A6 Queenzieburn

R
22 C1 Rackwick
24 B1 Raemoir
22 A2 Rapness
17 B6 Rathen
25 D4 Ratho
25 D4 Ratho Station
13 C4 Rattray
3 D5 Ravenglass
5 D6 Ravenscar
19 A5 Reay
5 C5 Redcar
15 B6 Redcastle
24 B2 Redcloak
3 B5 Red Dial
24 A1 Redhill
4 D3 Reeth
19 A6 Reiss
25 A4 Renfrew
4 B1 Renwick
23 D5 Rerwick
20 A2 Rhiconich
7 A5 Rhu
17 C4 Rhynie
4 D3 Richmond
24 B2 Rickarton
4 B3 Riding Mill
4 A2 Ridsdale
25 A6 Riggend
2 B3 Ringford
13 B6 Roadside Grm.
19 A5 Roadside Hgh.
22 A3 Roadside Ork.
8 D3 Roberton
5 D6 Robin Hood's Bay
9 D5 Rochester
20 D2 Rodel
8 B2 Romanno Bridge
5 D5 Rosedale Abbey
17 A6 Rosehearty
16 B1 Rosemarkie
7 A4 Roseneath
14 B1 Roskhill
8 B3 Roslin

25 C4 Rosyth
9 D5 Rothbury
16 B3 Rothes-on-Spey
7 B4 Rothesay
7 A5 Rowardennan
11 A5 Roybridge
8 A2 Rumbling Bridge
25 B4 Rutherglen
24 A3 Ruthrieston
13 C4 Ruthven

S
6 C3 Saddell
9 B5 St. Abb's
13 D5 St. Andrews
3 D4 St. Bees
11 D5 St. Catherines
17 B6 St. Combs
13 B6 St. Cyrus
25 C4 St. Davids
12 C2 St. Fillans
4 C2 St. John's Chapel
22 C2 St. Margarets Hope
22 C2 St. Mary's
13 D5 St. Monans
8 A1 St. Ninians
10 C3 Salen Str.
10 B3 Salen Hgh.
8 A2 Saline
24 C3 Salmond's Muir
7 C5 Saltcoats
6 B1 Sanaigmore
7 A4 Sandbank
2 B1 Sandhead
23 C4 Sandness
7 C4 Sannox
8 D1 Sanquhar
4 B3 Satley
24 A1 Sauchen
6 A1 Scalasaig
23 C5 Scalloway
19 A6 Scarfskerry
10 C1 Scarinish
14 C2 Sconser
4 D3 Scotch Corner
18 B2 Scourie
23 D5 Scousburgh
19 A5 Scrabster
9 C6 Seahouses
7 C4 Seamill
3 D5 Seascale
3 C5 Seatoller
4 D1 Sedbergh
8 C3 Selkirk
23 A5 Sellafirth
7 A5 Shandon
4 C1 Shap
21 A3 Shawbost
25 B5 Shettleston
15 C4 Shiel Bridge
14 B3 Shieldaig
4 C3 Shildon
4 B3 Shotley Bridge
8 B1 Shotts
3 B5 Silloth
4 A2 Simonburn
22 C2 Skaill
23 C5 Skellister
7 B4 Skelmorlie
3 C6 Skelton Cum.
5 C5 Skelton N.Y.
19 A4 Skerray
6 B3 Skipness
8 C2 Skirling
4 B2 Slaley
8 B1 Slamannan
5 D6 Sleights
14 C2 Sligachan Hotel
9 C4 Smailholm

3 B6 Smithfield
18 A3 Smoo
20 D1 Sollas
2 B2 Sorbie
7 C6 Sorn
4 D2 Soulby
25 A4 Southbar
9 D4 Southdean
6 D3 Southend
24 A1 South Kirkton
25 C4 South Queensferry
11 A5 Spean Bridge
5 C4 Spennymoor
16 A1 Spinningdale
9 B5 Spittal
12 B3 Spittal of Glenshee
25 A5 Springburn
3 A4 Springholm
9 C4 Sprouston
14 A2 Staffin
4 C3 Staindrop
7 C5 Stair
5 C5 Staithes
25 A6 Stand
8 B1 Stane
4 C3 Stanhope
12 C3 Stanley
4 A3 Stannington
3 B6 Stanwix
5 D4 Stapleton
3 D6 Staveley
14 B1 Stein
8 A1 Stenhousemuir
23 B4 Stenness
25 A5 Stepps
7 C5 Stevenston
7 C5 Stewarton
8 A1 Stirling
8 C2 Stobo
18 B1 Stoer
5 D4 Stokesley
25 B6 Stonefield
24 B2 Stonehaven
8 B1 Stonehouse
2 B1 Stoneykirk
24 A2 Stoneywood
21 B3 Stornoway
8 C3 Stow
13 A5 Strachan
7 A4 Strachur
7 D5 Straiton Str.

25 D6 Straiton Ltn.
12 B3 Straloch
2 B1 Stranraer
7 C6 Strathaven
7 A6 Strathblane
18 C2 Strathkanaird
13 D4 Strathmiglo
15 B6 Strathpeffer
19 A4 Strathy
12 D1 Strathyre
17 B6 Strichen
14 C3 Stromeferry
22 B1 Stromness
11 D6 Stronachlachar
7 A4 Strone
11 C5 Stronmilchan
11 B4 Strontian
12 B2 Struan
15 B5 Struy
24 B2 Sunnyside
9 B5 Swinton
23 B6 Symbister
7 C5 Symington Str.
8 C2 Symington Str.

T

16 A1 Tain
13 B5 Tannadice
25 B6 Tannochside
6 B3 Tarbert Str.
21 C2 Tarbert W.I.
11 D6 Tarbet
7 C5 Tarbolton
13 A5 Tarfside
17 D4 Tarland
14 D2 Tarskavaig
17 C5 Tarves
6 C3 Tayinloan
11 C4 Taynuilt
24 D2 Tayport
6 A3 Tayvallich
14 D3 Teangue
4 D1 Tebay
3 A5 Templand
8 B3 Temple
24 A2 Tertowie
8 C1 Thankerton
3 A4 Thornhill D.&G.
7 A6 Thornhill Cen.
25 B4 Thornliebank

8 A3 Thornton
9 D5 Thropton
3 B6 Thursby
19 A5 Thurso
20 D1 Tigharry
7 A4 Tighnabruaich
8 A1 Tillicoultry
10 B3 Tobermory
24 C1 Todhills
23 B5 Toft
25 B5 Tollcross
16 C2 Tomatin
11 A5 Tomdoun Hotel
16 C3 Tomintoul
16 C3 Tomnavoulin
2 B3 Tongland
18 A3 Tongue
15 C5 Torgyle
15 C6 Torness
8 B1 Torphichen
13 A5 Torphins
25 B5 Torrance Str.
25 A5 Torrance Str.
15 B4 Torridon
24 A3 Torry
8 A2 Torryburn
3 A5 Torthorwald
3 D5 Torver
14 C3 Toscaig
4 C3 Tow Law
8 B3 Tranent
19 A4 Trantlebeg
8 C3 Traquair
23 C5 Tresta
5 C4 Trimdon
12 C3 Trochry
7 C5 Troon
8 A1 Tullibody
7 D4 Turnberry
17 B5 Turriff
22 B1 Twatt
25 A6 Twechar
2 B3 Twynholm
11 C6 Tyndrum
3 A4 Tynron

U

25 B6 Uddingston
4 A3 Ugham
14 B2 Uig Hgh.

21 B2 Uig W.I.
3 C5 Uldale
15 A4 Ullapool
3 D5 Ulpha
23 B5 Ulsta
24 B2 Union Croft
25 D4 Uphall
25 D4 Uphall Station
24 B2 Upper Burnhaugh
24 B1 Upper Lochton
24 A3 Upper Tarbothill
24 C2 Upper Victoria
23 A6 Uyeasound

V

25 B6 Viewpark
23 D5 Virkie
23 B5 Voe

W

8 C3 Walkerburn
22 C1 Walls Ork.
23 C4 Walls She.
25 D6 Wallyford
8 D1 Wanlockhead
4 C2 Warcop
9 C6 Warenford
4 A2 Wark Nor.
9 C5 Wark Nor.
9 D6 Warkworth
22 B2 Wasbister
3 D6 Waterhead
12 C3 Waterloo
7 D5 Waterside
3 C4 Wath
19 A6 Watten
4 C2 Wear Head
12 B2 Weem
24 C2 Wellbank
3 B6 Welton
7 B4 Wemyss Bay
4 C3 West Auckland
8 B2 West Calder
24 A2 Wester Ord
24 B1 Westerton
24 A2 Westhill
7 B4 West Kilbride
8 B2 West Linton
24 B1 West Park

9 B4 Westruther
24 B2 Westside
6 B3 West Tarbert
3 B6 Wetheral
4 A3 Whalton
25 B6 Whifflet
8 B1 Whitburn
5 D6 Whitby
25 D6 Whitecraig
22 B2 Whitehall
3 C4 Whitehaven
17 B5 Whitehills
6 B3 Whitehouse
9 A4 Whitekirk
2 C2 Whithorn
7 C4 Whiting Bay
9 D5 Whittingham
4 B3 Whittonstall
19 A6 Wick
3 B5 Wigton
2 B2 Wigtown
25 D4 Wilkieston
4 C3 Willington
8 B1 Wilsontown
25 D4 Winchburgh
3 D6 Windermere
15 B6 Windhill
3 D6 Winster
4 C3 Winston
8 B1 Wishaw
4 C3 Witton-le-Wear
4 B3 Witton Gilbert
4 C3 Wolsingham
24 D1 Woodhaven
24 A3 Woodside
22 B2 Woodwick
9 C5 Wooler
3 C4 Workington
24 C3 Wormiehills
24 D1 Wormit

Y

22 B1 Yesnaby
9 C5 Yetholm
12 D3 Yetts of Muckart
25 A4 Yoker

Abbreviations used in city plan indexes

ber.	Aberdeen
ll.	Alley
pp.	Approach
r.	Arcade
v.	Avenue
dy.	Broadway
lds.	Buildings
ldgs.	Buildings
oul.	Boulevard
ri.	Bridge
ft.	Croft
irc.	Circus
lo.	Close
or.	Corner
otts.	Cottages
res.	Crescent
t.	Court
r.	Drive
ri.	Drive
	East
st.	Estate
dns.	Gardens
ra.	Grange
rn.	Green
ro.	Grove
o.	House
d.	Industrial
a.	Lane
	Lower
anno.	Mannofield
ans.	Mansions
kt.	Market
s.	Mews
t.	Mount
	North
th.	North
Aber.	Old Aberdeen
ar.	Parade
s.	Passage
.	Park
	Place
om.	Promenade
uad.	Quadrant
d.	Road
	Rise
	South
q.	Square
	Street
a.	Station
h.	South
r.	Terrace
d.	Trading
ls.	Villas
v.	View
.	West
f.	Wharf
k.	Walk
ood.	Woodside
.	Yard

street name followed by
e name of another street in
lics does not appear on the
ap but will be found
joining or near the latter.

ABERDEEN
32-35 Plan
36-37 Index

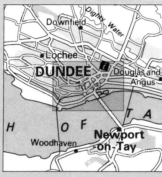

DUNDEE
38-39 Plan
40-41 Index

EDINBURGH
42-49 Plan
50-55 Index

GLASGOW
56-65 Plan
66-72 Index

ABERDEEN

DUNDEE

EDINBURGH

GLASGOW

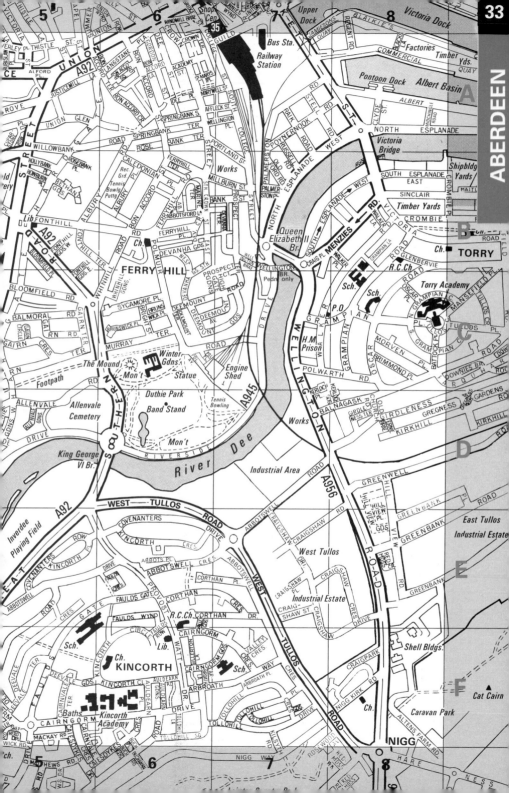

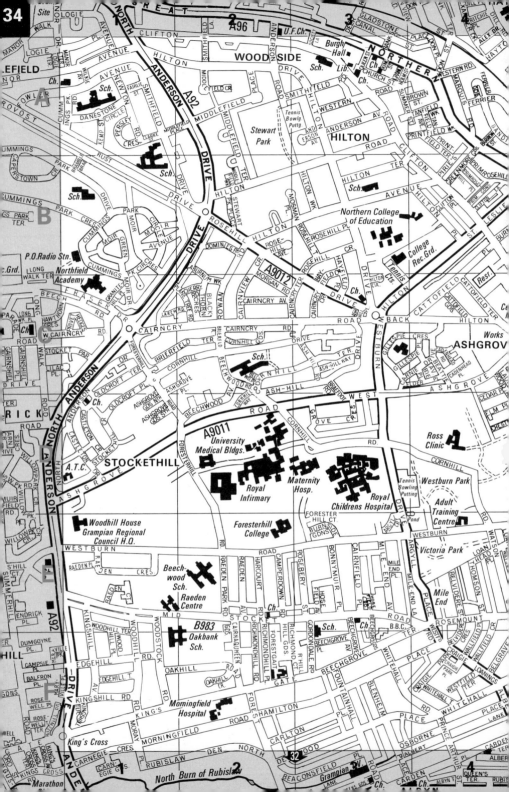

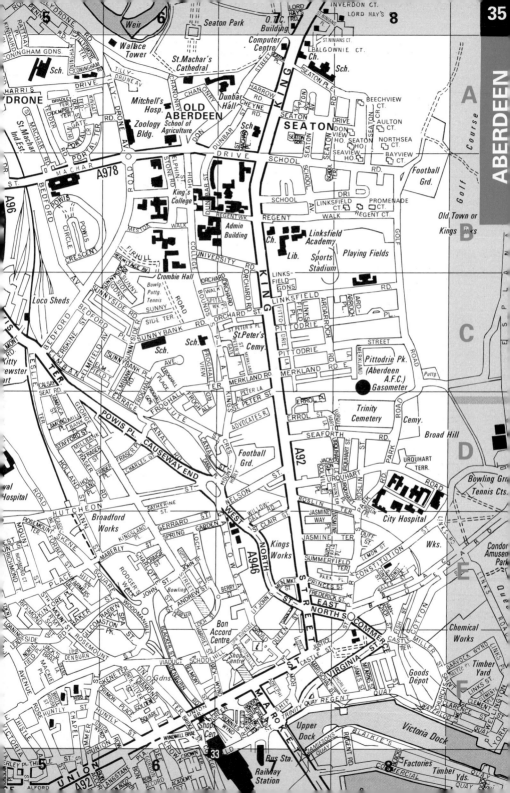

A
33 E6 Abbots Pl.
34 E3 Abbotsford La.
34 E3 Abbotsford Pl.
33 E7 Abbotswell Cres.
33 E5 Abbotswell Dr.
33 E7 Abbotswell Rd.
35 A8 Abergeldie Rd.
34 D2 Abergeldie Ter.
32 C4 Aboyne Gdns.
34 D1 Aboyne Pl.
32 F2 Aboyne Rd.
32 E2 Academy St.
33 A6 Adelphi
35 F7 Advocates Rd.
35 D7 Affleck St.
33 A6   Marywell St.
33 A6 Affleck St.
32 A3 Albert La.
34 F4 Albert Pl.
33 A8 Albert Quay
34 F4 Albert St.
32 A4 Albert Ter.
32 A4 Albert Wk.
     Albert Ter.
33 B6 Albury Pl.
33 B5 Albury Rd.
32 A4 Albyn Gro.
32 A4 Albyn Pl.
32 A4 Albyn Ter.
34 A4 Alexander Ter.
33 A5 Alford La.
     Alford Pl.
33 A5 Alford Pl.
32 B4 Allan St.
33 D5 Allenvale Gdns.
33 D5 Allenvale Rd.
33 F8 Altens Farm Rd.
34 A3 Anderson Av.
35 E5 Annat Bank
32 B3 Annfield Ter.
33 F6 Arbroath La.
33 F7 Arbroath Pl.
33 F6 Arbroath Way
35 C8 Ardarroch Pl.
35 C7 Ardarroch Rd.
34 E3 Argyll Cres.
34 E4 Argyll Pl.
34 C3 Ashgrove Ct.
     Back Hilton Rd.
34 D1 Ashgrove Gdns. N.
34 D1 Ashgrove Gdns. S.
34 C1 Ashgrove Pl.
34 C4 Ashgrove Rd.
34 D1 Ashgrove Rd. W.
34 C2 Ashill Dr.
34 C3 Ashill Pl.
34 C3 Ashill Rd.
34 C3 Ashill Way
32 B3 Ashley Gdns.
32 B3 Ashley La.
32 B4 Ashley Park Dr.
32 B3 Ashley Pk. N.
32 B4 Ashley Pk. S.
32 B4 Ashley Rd.
33 A5 Ashvale Ct.
     Cuparstone Row
32 A4 Ashvale Pl.
32 E2 Auchinyell Gdns.
32 F1 Auchinyell Rd.
32 E2 Auchinyell Ter.
35 C7 Auckland Pl.
     Merkland Pl.
33 F6 Auldearn Gdns.
33 F6 Auldearn Pl.
33 F6 Auldearn Rd.
35 A8 Aulton Cl.

B
34 C3 Back Hilton Rd.
35 F6 Back Wynd
35 E5 Baker Pl.
     Baker St.
35 E5 Baker St.
35 A7 Balgownie Ct.
33 C5 Balmoral Ct.
     South Mile-End
32 B4 Balmoral Pl.
32 C5 Balmoral Rd.
32 C4 Balmoral Ter.
33 B6 Bank St., Ferry Hill
34 A3 Bank St., Hilton
35 E8 Bannermill St.
     Cotton St.
34 A4 Barron St.
35 F6 Bath St.
     Windmill Brae
33 C8 Battock Pl.
35 A8 Bayview Ct.
32 A2 Bayview Rd.
32 B2 Bayview Rd. S.
35 E8 Beach Boulevard
32 A2 Beaconsfield Pl.
32 B4 Beattie Av.
34 C4 Beattie Pl.
35 B5 Bedford Av.
35 C5 Bedford Rd.

35 C5 Bedford Rd.
34 E3 Beechgrove Av.
34 E3 Beechgrove
     Gdns.
34 F3 Beechgrove Pl.
34 F3 Beechgrove Ter.
35 A8 Beechview Ct.
34 D2 Beechwood Av.
34 D1 Beechwood Ct.
     Castleton Dr.
34 C2 Beechwood Gdns.
34 C2 Beechwood Rd.
34 F4 Belgrave Ter.
35 C5 Belmont Rd.
35 F6 Belmont St.
34 F4 Belvidere Cres.
34 E4 Belvidere St.
35 E7 Berry St.
34 D4 Berryden Rd.
33 B5 Bethany Gdns.
34 C2 Birch Rd.
     Rowan Rd.
35 E6 Blackfriars St.
33 A8 Blacks La.
34 C2 Blackthorn Cres.
35 F8 Blaikies Quay
33 F3 Blenheim La.
33 B5 Blenheim Pl.
     Blenheim Pl.
33 B5 Bloomfield Pl.
33 C5 Bloomfield Rd.
33 C5 Bloomfield Rd.
35 C6 Boa Vista Pl.
     Spital
35 D8 Boddie Pl.
     Urquhart Rd.
33 A6 Bon Accord Cres.
33 A6 Bon Accord Cres.
     La.
     Bon Accord Cres.
33 A6 Bon Accord Sq.
33 A6 Bon Accord St.
33 A6 Bon Accord Ter.
34 E3 Bonnymuir Pl
35 A5 Bradley Ter.
34 C3 Braefoot Rd.
32 B4 Braemar Pl.
32 B4 Braeside Av.
32 D1 Braeside Ter.
34 B1 Bramble Brae
35 B6 Brewery La.
     High St.
35 F6 Bridge Pl.
     Bridge St.
35 F6 Bridge St.
34 C2 Brierfield Rd.
34 C1 Brierfield Ter.
35 C6 Bright St.
32 B3 Brighton Pl.
33 C8 Brimmond Pl.
35 F7 Broad St.
32 D4 Broomhill Av.
32 C4 Broomhill Pk.
     Broomhill Rd.
32 D4 Broomhill Pl.
35 A5 Broomhill Rd.
32 D4 Broomhill Rd.
34 C3 Brough Pl.
     Carnie Dr.
34 A4 Brown St.
35 C6 Brunswick Pl.
33 F6 Buchanan Pl.
34 B4 Burnett Pl.
32 B2 Burns Gdns.
32 B2 Burns Rd.
34 E3 Burnside Gdns.

C
34 C4 Cadenhead Pl.
34 C4 Cadenhead Rd.
33 F5 Caiesdykes Dr.
34 C2 Caircry Ter.
34 F2 Cairnaquheen
     Gdns.
34 C2 Cairncry Av.
34 C3 Cairncry Cres.
34 C1 Cairncry Ct.
     Brierfield Ter.
34 C2 Cairncry Rd.
34 E3 Cairnfield Pl., Mile
     End
33 F6 Cairngorm Cres.
33 F6 Cairngorm Gdns.
33 F5 Cairngorm Pl.
     Cairnvale Cres.
33 F5 Cairngorm Rd.
33 F5 Cairnvale Cres.
33 F5 Cairnvale Ter.
34 C2 Cairnview Cres.
33 B6 Caledonian La.
     Caledonian Pl.
33 B6 Caledonian Pl.
35 C5 Calsayseat Rd.
34 E2 Camperdown Rd.
35 D6 Canal Pl.
35 D6 Canal St.

35 D6 Canal St., Aber.
32 A3 Carden Pl.
32 A3 Carden Ter.
     Carden Pl.
34 F4 Carlton Pl.
35 F7 Carlton Pl.
     Carmelite La.
     Carmelite St.
35 F7 Carmelite St.
32 A1 Carnegie Cres.
32 A1 Carnegie Gdns.
35 F7 Carnegies Brae
     Flourmill La.
34 C3 Carnie Dr.
34 C3 Carnie Gdns.
     Carnie Dr.
35 E5 Caroline Pl.
35 E8 Castle Hill
     Hanover St.
35 F7 Castle St.
35 F7 Castle Ter.
34 D1 Castleton Cres.
34 D1 Castleton Dr.
     Castleton Dr.
34 D1 Castleton Dr.
35 D6 Catherine St.
34 C4 Cattofield Gdns.
34 C4 Cattofield Pl.
34 C4 Cattofield Ter.
35 D6 Causewayend
34 D4 Cedar Pl.
35 A6 Chanonry
35 F5 Chapel St.
35 D6 Charles St.
35 E6 Charlotte Pl.
     Charlotte St.
35 E6 Charlotte St.
32 B4 Chattan Pl.
34 C2 Cherry Rd.
34 D4 Chestnut Row
35 A7 Cheyne Rd.
34 A3 Church St.
     Woodside
35 F8 Church St.,
     Footdee
35 B6 Church Wk.
     High St.
32 B4 Claremont Gdns.
32 B4 Claremont Gro.
32 B4 Claremont Pl.
32 B4 Claremont St.
34 A1 Clarke St.
35 B6 Clarks La.
     Dunbar St.
34 B4 Clifton La.
34 B4 Clifton Pl.
33 A8 Clyde St.
35 B6 College Bounds
33 A6 College St.
35 D7 Colville Pl.
35 E8 Commerce St.
34 A8 Commercial Quay
35 F7 Concert Ct.
     Broad St.
35 A5 Coningham Gdns.
35 A5 Coningham Rd.
35 A5 Coningham Ter.
35 E8 Constitution La.
33 C8 Constitution St.
34 C1 Cornhill Ct.
     Brierfield Ter.
34 C2 Cornhill Gdns.
34 D3 Cornhill Rd.
34 C3 Cornhill Sq.
     Ashhill Rd.
34 C2 Cornhill Ter.
34 D2 Cornhill Way
33 A5 Correction Wynd
     St. Nicholas St.
33 E6 Corthan Cres.
33 E6 Corthan Dr.
33 E6 Corthan Pl.
32 B4 Cottage Brae
35 E8 Cotton St.
33 E6 Covenanters Dr.
35 E5 Covenanters Row
33 B6 Craibstone La.
     Bon Accord St.
33 B7 Craig Pl.
32 C2 Craigie Lea Av.
34 F4 Craigie Loanings
34 F4 Craigie Park Pl.
34 F4 Craigie Pk.
32 E2 Craigievar Cres.
32 E2 Craigievar Pl.
32 E2 Craigievar Rd.
     Montrose Dr.
32 F3 Craigievar Ter.
33 F8 Craigpark
33 E7 Craigshaw Cres.
33 E7 Craigshaw Dr.
33 E7 Craigshaw Rd.
33 E7 Craigshaw St.
32 D1 Craigton Av.
32 D2 Craigton Ct.
32 D1 Craigton Rd.

32 D1 Craigton Ter.,
     Aber.
32 D3 Cranford Pl.
32 D2 Cranford Rd.
32 D2 Cranford Ter.
33 D5 Crathie Gardens
     W.
33 D5 Crathie Ter.
35 F6 Crimon Pl.
33 B8 Crombie Rd.
32 B3 Cromwell Ct.,
     Forbesfield Rd.
32 B2 Cromwell Gdns.
32 B2 Cromwell Rd.
33 A6 Crown La.
     Crown Ter.
33 A6 Crown St.
33 A6 Crown Ter., Aber.
34 B1 Cummings Pk.
     Circle
34 A1 Cummings Pk. Rd.
33 A5 Cuparstone Row
33 B5 Cuparstone La.
     Cuparstone Row
33 B5 Cuparstone La.
     Great Western Rd.
33 B5 Cuparstone Row

D
34 A1 Danestone Circle
33 A6 Dee Pl.
33 A6 Dee St.
35 A5 Deemount Av.
35 D6 Deemount Gdns.
35 D5 Deemount Rd.
35 D5 Deemount Ter.
32 E1 Deeside Av.
32 E1 Deeside Cres.
32 E1 Deeside Dr.
32 E1 Deeside Gdns.
32 E1 Deeside Pk.
32 E1 Deeside Pl.
32 E1 Deeside Ter.
33 F5 Deevale Cres.
33 F5 Deevale Gdns.
33 F5 Deevale Rd.
33 F5 Deevale Ter.
35 A5 Dempsey Ter.
35 F6 Denburn Rd.
32 A2 Desswood Pl.
33 C5 Devanha Cres.
33 C5 Devanha Gdns.
33 C5 Devanha Gdns. E.
33 C5 Devanha Gdns. S.
33 C5 Devanha Gdns. W.
33 C5 Devanha La.
     Devanha Gdns.
33 B7 Devanha Ter.
32 F2 Devenick Pl.
32 B3 Devonshire Rd.
33 A5 Diamond La.
     Union St.
35 F6 Diamond Pl.
     Union Ter.
35 F6 Diamond St.
34 B2 Dominies Rd.
34 A4 Don Pl., Wood.
35 E5 Donald Pl.
     Forbes St.
33 A8 Donview Ho.
35 B6 Douglas La.
     High St.
35 E8 Duff St.
35 B6 Dunbar St.
35 B6 Duncans Pl.
     High St.
32 C2 Duthie Ct.
     Duthie Ter.
32 D2 Duthie Pl.
32 C2 Duthie Ter.

E
32 A3 Earls Court Gdns.
33 B6 East Craibstone St.
     Bon Accord St.
35 F7 East Grn.
     Hadden St.
35 E7 East North St.
35 E5 Eden Pl.
34 F1 Edgehill Rd.
34 F1 Edgehill Ter.
34 C4 Elder Pl.
34 D4 Elm Pl.
35 C6 Elmbank Rd.
35 C5 Elmbank Ter.
35 C5 Elmfield Av.
34 C5 Elmfield Ter.
35 D7 Elphinstone Rd.
35 D7 Errol Pl.
35 D7 Errol St.
34 E4 Esslemont Av.
35 F7 Exchange La.
     Exchange St.
35 F7 Exchange St.

35 F7 Exchequer Row
     Shiprow

F
34 A1 Fairlie St.
35 E5 Farmers Hall La.
35 E7 Farrier La.
     Mealmarket St.
33 E6 Faulds Cres.
33 F5 Faulds Gate
33 F6 Faulds Row
33 E6 Faulds Wynd
33 D8 Fernie Brae
34 A4 Ferrier Cres.
34 A4 Ferrier Gdns.
33 B6 Ferryhill Pl.
33 B6 Ferryhill Rd.
33 B6 Ferryhill Ter.
35 B6 Firhill Rd.
35 E8 Fish St.
35 F7 Flourmill La.
33 B5 Fonthill Gdns. E.
33 B5 Fonthill Gdns. W.
33 B5 Fonthill Rd.
33 B5 Fonthill Ter.
35 E5 Forbes St.
32 B3 Forbesfield La.
32 B3 Forbesfield Rd.
32 B3 Forest Av.
34 F2 Forest Rd.
34 A3 Foresterhill Ct.
34 C1 Foresterhill Rd.
34 F2 Forestgait
35 A5 Formartine Rd.
34 F3 Fountainhall Rd.
35 D6 Fraser Pl.
35 D5 Fraser Rd.
35 D5 Fraser St.
35 E7 Frederick St.
35 D6 Froghall Av.
35 D6 Froghall Gdns.
35 D6 Froghall Pl.
35 D6 Froghall Rd.
35 C6 Froghall Ter.
35 D6 Froghall Vw.
32 C2 Fullerton Ct.
     Great Western Rd.

G
35 F6 Gaelic La.
     Belmont St.
33 C5 Gairn Circle
33 C5 Gairn Cres.
33 C5 Gairn Ct.
     Gairn Ter.
33 C5 Gairn Ter.
32 F1 Gaitside Cres.
32 E2 Gaitside Dr.
32 F1 Gaitside Pl.
32 E2 Gaitside Rd.
32 F1 Gaitside Ter.
35 F7 Gallowgate
32 E2 Garthdee Cres.
32 E2 Garthdee Dr.
32 E2 Garthdee Gdns.
     Garthdee Ter.
32 F1 Garthdee Rd.
32 E3 Garthdee Ter.
35 D5 George St.
35 E6 Gerrard St.
35 F5 Gilcomston Ct.
     Kidd St.
35 F5 Gilcomston Land
     Kidd St.
35 F5 Gilcomston Pk.
35 E5 Gilcomston Ter.
     Farmers Hall La.
34 C3 Gillespie Cres.
32 F1 Gillespie Pl.
33 D8 Girdleness Rd.
33 D8 Girdleness Ter.
32 A3 Gladstone Pl.,
     Mannofield
33 B8 Glenbervie Rd.
35 F6 Golden Sq.
35 B8 Golf Rd., Aber.
32 D1 Gordon Rd.,
     Manno.
34 A6 Gordon St.
32 D2 Gordon Ter.,
     Manno.
34 F3 Gordondale Ct.
     Gordondale Rd.
34 F3 Gordondale Rd.
33 B8 Grampian La.
33 C8 Grampian Pl.
33 D8 Grampian Rd.
34 A3 Grandholm St.
34 C1 Granitehill Pl.
32 A4 Granton St.
35 B6 Grants Pl.
     High St.
32 C3 Granville Pl.
32 C3 Gray St.
     Great Southern Rd.
32 A4 Great Western Pl.

32 C2 Great Western Rd.
35 F7 Green
33 E8 Greenbank Cres.
33 E8 Greenbank Pl.
33 E8 Greenbank Rd.
34 B4 Greenmore Gdns.
33 D8 Greenwell Rd.
35 E5 Greig Ct.
     Hutcheon St.
34 F4 Grosvenor Pl.
34 D3 Grove Cres.
33 A7 Guild St.

H
35 F7 Hadden St.
34 F2 Hamilton Pl.
32 C2 Hammerfield Av.
32 C3 Hammersmith Rd.
35 E8 Hanover St.
34 E2 Harcourt Rd.
33 B5 Hard Gate
32 B2 Harlaw Pl.
32 B2 Harlaw Rd.
32 B2 Harlaw Ter.
35 F6 Harriet St.
35 A5 Harris Dr.
34 A7 Harrow Rd.
32 A4 Hartington Rd.
35 D8 Hawthorn Ter.
     Urquhart Pl.
34 C3 Hayfield Cres.
34 B3 Hayfield Pl.
34 A4 Hayton Rd.
32 E4 Headland Ct.
34 B6 Hermitage Av.
35 F5 Hetherwick Rd.
35 B6 High St.
33 C7 Highgate Gdns.
35   Hill St.
34 D8 Hill View Gdns.
33 D8 Hill View Pl.
33 D8 Hill Vw. Wd. Rd.
35 C6 Hillhead Ter.
     Spital
34 B2 Hilton Av.
35 B6 Hilton Circle
34 B2 Hilton Ct.
     Stewart Park Pl.
34 A3 Hilton Dr.
34 B4 Hilton Pl.
34 B2 Hilton Rd.
34 C3 Hilton St.
34 B3 Hilton Ter.
34 B4 Hilton Wk.
32 C5 Holburn Pl.
32 C5 Holburn Rd.
32 E4 Holburn St.
32 D5 Holland Pl.
35 D5 Holland St.
33 B5 Hollybank Pl.
34 E3 Hosefield Av.
34 E3 Hosefield Rd.
33 B5 Howburn Pl.
35 D8 Hunter Pl.
35 F5 Huntly St.
35 E5 Hutcheon Ct.
     Hutcheon St.
35 E5 Hutcheon St.
32 D2 Hutchison Ter.

I
35 F7 Imperial Pl.
     Stirling St.
32 F1 Inchbrae Dr.
32 F2 Inchbrae Rd.
32 F1 Inchbrae Ter.
32 B4 Irvine Pl.
32 E2 Ivanhoe Pl.
32 F1 Ivanhoe Rd.
32 E1 Ivanhoe Wk.

J
35 F5 Jacks Brae
35 D7 Jackson Ter.
35 D5 Jamaica St.
35 F8 James St.
35 F7 Jamiesons Quay
32 C3 Jasmine Pl.
35 E7 Jasmine Ter.
35 E7 Jasmine Way
35 E6 John St., Aber.
35 E6 Jopps La.
33 A5 Justice Mill Brae
     Justice Mill La.
33 A5 Justice Mill La.
35 F7 Justice St.
35 D6 Jute St.

K
32 E3 Kaimhill Circle
32 E3 Kaimhill Gdns.
32 E3 Kaimhill Rd.
34 A1 Kemp St.
32 E3 Kenfield Cres.
32 C1 Kenfield Pl.

2 B1 Kepplestone Av.
3 C8 Kerloch Gdns.
3 C7 Kerloch Pl.
5 F5 Kidd St.
3 F7 Kilsyth Rd.
3 F6 Kincorth Circle
3 E6 Kincorth Cres.
3 E6 Kincorth Gdns.
Kincorth Cres.
3 E5 Kincorth Pl.
3 D6 King George VI Br.
5 C7 King St., Aber.
4 A3 King St., Wood.
5 D7 Kings Cres.
4 E1 Kingshill Av.
4 F1 Kingshill Rd.
4 F1 Kingshill Ter.
5 E6 Kingsland Pl.
5 E5 Kintore Gdns.
Kintore Pl.
5 E5 Kintore Pl.
3 D8 Kirkhill Rd., Aber.

L

4 B2 Laburnum Wk.
5 D5 Lamond Pl.
3 A6 Langstane Pl.
4 C1 Larch Rd.
4 C4 Laurel Wood Av.
5 F5 Leadside Rd.
2 B3 Learney Pl.
2 F4 Leggart Av.
2 F4 Leggart Cres.
2 F4 Leggart Pl.
2 F4 Leggart Rd.
2 F4 Leggart Ter.
5 E8 Lemon Pl.
Park St.
5 E8 Lemon St.
4 B4 Leslie Rd.
5 C5 Leslie Ter.
4 B4 Lilybank Pl.
5 F6 Lindsay St.
Golden Sq.
5 B7 Linksfield Ct.
5 C7 Linksfield Gdns.
5 C7 Linksfield Pl.
5 C7 Linksfield Rd.
5 F6 Little Belmont St.
Belmont St.
5 F5 Little Chapel St.
Chapel St.
5 E7 Little John St.
4 E4 Loanhead Pl.
4 E4 Loanhead Ter.
4 E4 Loanhead Wk.
Loanhead Ter.
5 E6 Loch St.
5 F7 Lodge Wk.
2 B2 Louisville Av.

M

5 E6 Maberley St.
3 F5 Mackay Rd.
5 B6 Mackenzie Pl.
High St.
5 F5 Mackie Pl.
5 E5 Magdala Pl.
Short Loanings
4 A1 Manor Ter.
2 D4 Margaret Pl.
Ruthrieston Circle
5 F5 Margaret St.
Rose St.
3 B6 Marine Ct.
Marine Ter.
3 B6 Marine Ter.
5 F7 Marischal Ct.
Justice St.
5 F7 Marischal St.
5 B6 Market La.
High St.
5 F7 Market St., Aber.
4 A4 Marquis Rd.
5 F7 Martins La.
Carmelite St.
3 A6 Marywell St.
2 B2 Mayfield Gdns.
3 A5 McCombies Ct.
Netherkirkgate
5 E7 Mealmarket St.
5 F8 Mearns St.
3 C7 Menzies Rd.
5 C8 Merkland La.
5 C7 Merkland Pl.
5 C7 Merkland Rd.
5 C7 Merkland Rd. E.
5 B6 Meston Wk.
4 E2 Mid Stocket Rd.
3 A8 Midchingle Rd.
4 A2 Middlefield Cres.
4 A2 Middlefield Pl.
4 A2 Middlefield Ter.
34 B2 Middlefield Wk.
34 E3 Mile End Av.
34 E3 Mile End La.
34 E3 Mile End Pl.
35 D5 Millbank La.
35 D5 Millbank Pl.
33 B6 Millburn St.
35 F8 Miller St.
35 F5 Minister La.
34 B1 Moir Av.
34 B1 Moir Cres.
34 C1 Moir Dr.
34 B1 Moir Grn.
32 F2 Montrose Dr.
34 F1 Moray Pl.
34 C2 Morgan Rd.
34 F1 Morningfield Rd.
32 E2 Morningside Av.
32 E2 Morningside Cres.
32 D2 Morningside Gdns.
32 D2 Morningside Pl.
32 D2 Morningside Rd.
32 D2 Morningside Ter.
32 F1 Morrison Dr.
33 C8 Morven Pl.
34 A2 Mosman Pl.
35 D7 Mount Hooly
35 E5 Mount St.
32 A4 Murray Ct.
Great Western Rd.
33 C6 Murray Ter.

N

32 B4 Nellfield Pl.
35 D7 Nelson La.
Nelson St.
35 D7 Nelson St.
33 A5 Netherkirkgate
Union St.
32 D3 Newlands Av.
32 D3 Newlands Cres.
34 A1 Newton Rd., Aber.
33 A5 Nicholas La.
St. Nicholas St.
33 F8 Nigg Kirk Rd.
32 D3 Norfolk Rd.
33 A8 North Esplanade E.
33 B7 North Esplanade W.
33 C8 North Grampian Circ.
35 F6 North Silver St.
35 E6 North St. Andrew St.
St. Andrew St.
35 F5 Northfield Pl.
35 A8 Northsea Ct.
35 E5 Novar Pl.
Ann St.

O

32 D2 Oakdale Ter.
34 F2 Oakhill Cres.
34 F1 Oakhill Rd.
33 D8 Old Church Rd.
33 B7 Old Ford Rd.
34 D1 Oldcroft Ct.
Castleton Dr.
34 D1 Oldcroft Pl.
34 C1 Oldcroft Ter.
33 B6 Oldmill Rd.
Bon Accord St.
35 C7 Orchard La.
Orchard Pl.
35 C7 Orchard Pl.
35 C7 Orchard Rd.
35 C7 Orchard St.
35 C6 Orchard Wk.
34 F3 Osborne Pl.
33 C8 Oscar Pl.
33 C8 Oscar Rd.

P

33 B7 Palmerston Pl.
33 B7 Palmerston Rd.
35 E7 Park Pl.
35 D8 Park Rd., Aber.
35 E8 Park St.
35 F6 Patagonian Ct.
Belmont St.
35 E7 Peacocks Clo.
East North St.
34 A1 Persley Cres.
34 B4 Piries La.
32 E3 Pitmedden Cres.
32 E3 Pitmedden Rd., Aber.
32 E3 Pitmedden Ter.
32 B4 Pitstruan Pl.
32 C4 Pitstruan Ter.
35 C7 Pittodrie La.
35 C7 Pittodrie Pl.
35 C7 Pittodrie St.
34 C2 Plane Tree Rd.
33 C6 Polmuir Av.
33 C6 Polmuir Pl.
33 B6 Polmuir Rd.
33 C7 Polwarth Rd.
34 C1 Poplar Rd.
Larch Rd.
35 A5 Portal Cres.
35 B5 Portal Ter.
35 E7 Porthill Ct.
Gallowgate
33 A6 Portland St.
35 F7 Poultry Market La.
Queen St.
35 B5 Powis Circle
35 B5 Powis Cres.
35 D6 Powis Pl.
35 C5 Powis Ter.
33 A7 Poynernook Rd.
34 B4 Primrosehill Dr.
34 B4 Primrosehill Gdns.
34 B4 Primrosehill Pl.
34 F4 Prince Arthur St.
35 E7 Princes St.
34 A4 Printfield Ter.
34 A4 Printfield Wk.
34 C1 Privet Hedges
35 B8 Promenade Ct.
33 C6 Prospect Ct.
33 B7 Prospect Ter.
33 E6 Provost Watt Dr.

Q

35 F7 Queen St., Aber.
34 A3 Queen St., Hilton
32 B1 Queens Av.
32 B2 Queens Ct.
32 A3 Queens Gdns.
32 A3 Queens La. N.
32 A3 Queens La. S.
32 A4 Queens Ter.

R

35 E6 Raeburn Pl.
34 E2 Raeden Av.
34 E1 Raeden Cres.
34 E1 Raeden Ct.
34 E2 Raeden Pk. Rd.
34 E1 Raeden Pl.
33 A7 Raik Rd.
32 E2 Ramsay Cres.
32 F2 Ramsay Gdns.
32 F2 Ramsay Pl.
33 E8 Red Moss Cres.
35 B8 Regent Ct.
35 F8 Regent Quay
35 F8 Regent Rd.
35 B7 Regent Wk.
35 F5 Rennies Wynd
35 E5 Richmond Ct.
35 E5 Richmond St.
35 E5 Richmond Ter.
35 E5 Richmond Wk.
34 F3 Richmondhill Ct.
34 F2 Richmondhill Gdns.
34 F2 Richmondhill Pl.
34 F2 Richmondhill Rd.
33 D6 Riverside Dr.
33 D5 Riverside Ter.
35 E6 Rodgers Wk.
35 F5 Rose Pl.
Rose St.
35 F5 Rose St.
33 B5 Rosebank Pl.
33 A6 Rosebank Ter.
34 E3 Rosebery St.
34 B2 Rosehill Av.
34 B3 Rosehill Cres.
34 C1 Rosehill Ct.
Brierfield Ter.
34 B2 Rosehill Dr.
34 B3 Rosehill Pl.
34 B3 Rosehill Ter.
34 E4 Rosemount Pl.
35 E5 Rosemount Sq.
35 E5 Rosemount Ter.
35 F5 Rosemount Viaduct
35 D8 Roslin Pl.
35 D8 Roslin St.
35 D7 Roslin Ter.
34 C2 Rowan Rd.
32 A1 Royfold Cres.
32 A1 Rubislaw Den Gdns.
32 A1 Rubislaw Den N.
32 A1 Rubislaw Den S.
32 A4 Rubislaw Pl.
32 A4 Rubislaw Ter.
32 A4 Rubislaw Terrace La.
Rubislaw Ter.
35 F6 Ruby La.
North Silver St.
35 F6 Ruby Pl.
North Silver St.
33 A7 Russell Rd.
32 E4 Ruth Gdns.
32 D3 Ruthrie Gdns.
32 E3 Ruthrie Rd.
32 E3 Ruthrie Ter.
32 D4 Ruthrieston Circle
32 D4 Ruthrieston Cres.
32 D4 Ruthrieston Pl.
32 D3 Ruthrieston Rd.

S

35 E6 St. Andrew St.
33 A5 St. Catharines Wynd
Union St.
35 E7 St. Clair St.
33 A6 St. Johns Pl.
Academy St.
32 D1 St. Johns Ter.
35 B5 St. Machar Dr.
35 A7 St. Machar Pl.
35 A5 St. Machar Rd.
33 A6 St. Marys Pl., Aber.
33 A5 St. Nicholas La.
Union St.
33 A5 St. Nicholas St.
Union St.
35 A7 St. Ninians Ct.
35 E7 St. Paul St.
Gallowgate
35 D7 St. Peter La.
35 D7 St. Peter St.
35 C7 St. Peters Gate
35 C7 St. Peters Pl.
32 A3 St. Swithin St.
32 C3 Salisbury Ct.
Salisbury Ter.
32 C4 Salisbury Pl.
32 C3 Salisbury Ter.
34 A4 Sandiland Dr.
35 B7 School Av.
35 B7 School Dr.
35 F6 School Hill
35 B7 School Rd., Seaton
35 B7 School Ter.
35 B8 School Wk.
32 B1 Seafield Av.
32 C1 Seafield Cres.
32 C1 Seafield Ct.
32 B1 Seafield Dr. E.
32 C1 Seafield Dr. W.
32 C1 Seafield Gdns.
32 C1 Seafield Rd.
35 D7 Seaforth Rd.
35 E7 Seamount Ct.
Gallowgate
35 E7 Seamount Rd.
Gallowgate
35 A7 Seaton Av.
35 A8 Seaton Cres.
35 A7 Seaton Dr.
35 A7 Seaton Gdns.
35 A8 Seaton Ho.
35 A7 Seaton Pl.
35 A7 Seaton Pl. E.
35 A7 Seaton Rd.
35 A7 Seaton Wk.
35 A8 Seaview Ho.
33 F5 Shepherd Pl.
35 F7 Ship Row
35 E7 Shoe La.
35 F7 Shore Brae
Shiprow
35 F8 Shore La.
35 E5 Short Loanings
33 F6 Sillerton La.
33 B8 Sinclair Rd.
35 F5 Skene La.
35 E5 Skene Sq.
35 F5 Skene St.
35 F6 Skene Ter.
34 A1 Smithfield Ct.
Fairlie St.
34 A1 Smithfield Dr.
34 A2 Smithfield La.
34 A3 Smithfield Rd.
34 A3 Society La.
32 C3 South Anderson Dr.
33 A7 South College St.
35 E8 South Constitution St.
33 B6 South Crown St.
33 B8 South Esplanade E.
33 B7 South Esplanade W.
33 C8 South Grampian Circ.
33 C5 South Mile End
35 E5 South Mount St.
33 A5 South Silver St.
Union St.
34 C2 South Wk.
Ashhill Dr.
35 E6 Spa St.
32 A2 Spademill La.
32 A2 Spademill Rd.
35 C6 Spital
35 C6 Spital Wk.
35 E6 Spring Gdn.
33 A6 Springbank Pl.
Bon Accord St.
33 A6 Springbank St.
33 A6 Springbank Ter.
32 C1 Springfield Rd.
35 D5 Stafford St.
32 A3 Stanley St.
33 A7 Stell Rd.
35 F5 Stevenson St.
Leadside Rd.
34 B2 Stewart Park Ct.
Stewart Park Pl.
34 B2 Stewart Park Pl.
35 F7 Stirling St.
34 D1 Stockethill Av.
Stockethill Cres.
34 D1 Stockethill Cres.
34 C1 Stockethill Ct.
Foresterhill Rd.
34 C1 Stockethill La.
Oldcroft Ter.
34 D1 Stockethill Pl.
Castleton Dr.
34 D1 Stockethill Sq.
Stockethill Cres.
34 C1 Stockethill Way
Oldcroft Ter.
35 F8 Sugarhouse La.
Mearns St.
35 F5 Summer St., Aber.
34 A3 Summer St., Hilton
35 E7 Summerfield Pl.
35 E7 Summerfield Ter.
35 C6 Sunnybank Pl.
35 C6 Sunnybank Rd.
35 C6 Sunnyside Av.
35 C6 Sunnyside Gdns.
35 C6 Sunnyside Rd.
35 C6 Sunnyside Ter.
35 C6 Sunnyside Wk.
Sunnybank Pl.
33 C6 Sycamore Pl.

T

32 F1 Talisman Dr.
32 F1 Talisman Rd.
32 E1 Talisman Wk.
34 A4 Tanfield Av.
34 A4 Tanfield Ct.
Tanfield Wk.
34 A4 Tanfield Wk.
35 A5 Tedder Rd.
35 A5 Tedder St.
35 F8 Theatre La.
Regent Quay
35 F5 Thistle Ct.
Rose St.
35 F5 Thistle La.
33 A5 Thistle Pl.
Thistle St.
33 A5 Thistle St.
35 B6 Thoms Ct.
High St.
35 B6 Thoms Pl.
High St.
34 E4 Thomson St.
32 C2 Thorngrove Av.
32 C2 Thorngrove Ct.
35 A6 Tillydrone Av.
35 A5 Tillydrone Ter.
33 F7 Tollohill Cres.
33 F7 Tollohill Dr.
33 F7 Tollohill Gdns.
33 F6 Tollohill La.
33 F7 Tollohill Pl.
33 F6 Tollohill Sq.
35 F7 Trinity La.
Exchange St.
35 F7 Trinity Quay
35 F7 Trinity St.
33 C8 Tullos Circle
32 F3 Two Mile Cross

U

35 F6 Union Bri.
33 A5 Union Glen
32 B3 Union Gro.
32 A4 Union Gro. La.
32 B3 Union Grove Ct.
Union Gro.
33 A5 Union Row
33 A5 Union St.
35 F6 Union Ter.
35 F5 Union Wynd
35 B6 University Rd.
35 F5 Upper Denburn
35 F7 Upper Kirkgate
35 D8 Urquhart La.
35 D8 Urquhart Pl.
35 D8 Urquhart Rd.
35 D8 Urquhart St.
35 D8 Urquhart Ter.

V

33 F7 Valley Cres.
33 E6 Valley Gdns.
33 A8 Victoria Bri.
33 B8 Victoria Rd.
35 F5 Victoria St., Aber.
35 E5 View Ter.
32 C1 Viewfield Av.
32 C1 Viewfield Cres.
32 C1 Viewfield Rd.
35 F7 Virginia Ct.
Justice St.
35 F8 Virginia St.

W

35 B6 Wagrills La.
High St.
35 F8 Wales La.
Mearns St.
35 E8 Wales St.
33 B8 Walker La.
33 B8 Walker Pl.
33 C7 Walker Rd.
34 F4 Wallfield Cres.
34 F4 Wallfield Pl.
35 F8 Water La.
Mearns St.
35 F8 Waterloo Quay
34 E4 Watson La.
34 E4 Watson St.
35 F5 Waverley La.
33 A5 Waverley Pl.
33 F5 Webster Rd.
35 F8 Weighhouse Sq.
Virginia St.
32 C1 Wellbrae Ter.
33 B7 Wellington Brae
33 B7 Wellington Bridge
33 A6 Wellington Pl.
33 C7 Wellington Rd., Aber.
33 A6 West Craibstone St.
Bon Accord Ter.
35 E5 West Mount St.
35 E7 West North St.
33 D6 West Tullos Rd.
34 E1 Westburn Ct.
Westburn Rd.
34 C3 Westburn Dr.
34 E1 Westburn Rd.
34 A3 Western Rd.
34 F4 Westfield Rd.
34 F4 Westfield Ter.
33 C6 Whinhill Gdns.
33 C6 Whinhill Rd.
34 F4 Whitehall Pl.
34 F3 Whitehall Rd.
34 F4 Whitehall Ter.
35 F5 Whitehouse St.
34 A1 Wilkie Av.
33 A5 Willowbank Rd.
35 E7 Willowdale Rd.
35 F6 Windmill Brae
35 F6 Windmill La.
Windmill Brae
35 F5 Windsor Pl.
Victoria St.
35 A5 Wingate Pl.
35 A5 Wingate Rd.
34 D1 Woodhill Ct.
Castleton Dr.
34 F1 Woodhill Pl.
34 F1 Woodhill Rd.
34 E1 Woodhill Ter.
34 F1 Woodstock Rd.
35 E6 Woolmanhill
35 B6 Wright & Coopers Pl.
High St.

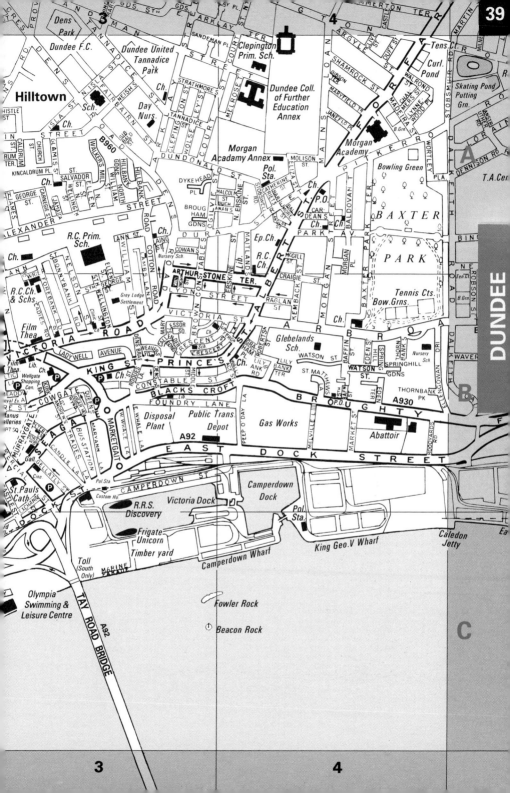

DUNDEE

A
38 A2 Adelaide Pl.
38 A2 Adelaide Ter.
38 C2 Airlie Pl.
38 A1 Albany Ter.
39 B3 Albert Sq.
39 B4 Albert St.
39 A3 Alexander St.
39 B3 Allan St.
38 A2 Alva Sq.
38 B1 Anchor La.
39 A3 Ann St.
38 B1 Annfield Rd.
38 B1 Annfield Row
38 B1 Annfield St.
39 B4 Arbroath Rd.
39 A4 Argyle St.
39 A3 Arklay St.
38 B2 Arthur St.
39 A3 Arthurstone Ter.
38 C2 Artillery La.
38 B2 Ash St.

B
39 B4 Baffin St.
39 B4 Baffin Ter.
   Baffin St.
39 A4 Baldovan Ter.
38 A1 Balgayview
   Gdns.
39 A4 Balmore St.
38 C1 Baltic Gdns.
   Patons La.
39 B3 Baltic La.
38 B1 Bank Mill Rd.
38 B2 Bank St.
38 B2 Barrack Rd.
38 B2 Barrack St.
39 B4 Baxter Park Ter.
38 A1 Baxter St.
38 B2 Bell St.
38 C1 Bellefield Av.
38 B1 Bellfield St.
38 A1 Benvie Rd.
38 A1 Black St.
38 B1 Blackness St.
39 B3 Blacks Croft
38 B2 Blinshall St.
38 A1 Blyth Pl.
38 A1 Blyth St.
39 A3 Bonnybank Rd.
38 B1 Brewery La.
39 A3 Brougham Gdns.
39 B4 Broughty Ferry Rd.
39 B3 Brown Constable St.
38 B2 Brown St., Dun.
38 A2 Bruce St.
39 A4 Buchanan St.
38 A2 Burgess St.
38 A2 Butterburn Sq.

C
39 A3 Caldrum St.
39 B3 Callender Gdns.
38 A1 Campbell St.
39 B3 Camperdown St.,
   Dun.
39 B3 Candle La.
39 A4 Cardean St.
38 A2 Carmichael St.
39 A3 Carnegie St.
39 B3 Castle St., Dun.
39 A4 Catherine St.
39 A4 Chalmers St.

39 A3 Church St., Dun.
38 A1 City Rd.
39 B3 City Sq.
38 A1 Cleghorn St.
39 A3 Clepington St.
39 A4 Clive St.
38 A1 Cobden Pl.
39 B3 Commercial St.
39 B3 Constable St.
38 B2 Constitution Rd.
38 A2 Constitution Ter.
38 B1 Corso St.
39 A3 Cotton Rd.
38 B2 Court House Sq.
39 A3 Court St.
39 A4 Court St. N.
38 C2 Coutties Wynd
39 A3 Cowan St.
39 B3 Cowgate
38 C2 Craig Pier
39 B4 Craigie St.
39 B3 Crescent La.
39 B3 Crescent St.
38 B2 Crichton St.
38 B2 Cross La.
38 B2 Cross Row
39 B3 Cunningham St.

D
38 B1 Daniel St.
39 B3 Dens Brae
39 A3 Dens Rd.
39 B3 Dens St.
38 A2 Derby St.
39 B3 Dock St.
38 A2 Dons Rd.
38 B1 Douglas St.
38 A2 Douglas Ter., Dun.
38 A2 Drummond St.
38 B2 Dudhope Crescent
   Rd.
38 A1 Dudhope Ct.
38 B2 Dudhope St.
38 A1 Dudhope Ter.
38 A4 Duff St.
38 A2 Dunblane Pl.
39 A3 Dundonald St.
39 A3 Dura St.
39 A3 Dykehead Pl.

E
39 B3 Eadies Rd.
39 C3 Earl Grey Pl.
38 B1 Eassons Angle
39 B3 East Dock St.
38 B2 East Hendersons
   Wynd
38 A2 East Somerville Pl.
39 B3 East Whale La.
39 B4 Eden St.
39 B4 Eden Ter.
38 B1 Edward St.
39 A4 Eliza St.
39 A3 Ellen St.
39 B4 Ellengowan Dr.
39 A4 Erskine St.
38 B2 Euclid Cres.
38 B2 Euclid St.
39 B3 Exchange St.

F
39 A3 Fairbairn St.

39 B4 Ferguson St.
38 A2 Fingask St.
38 B1 Fleuchar St.
38 B1 Fords La.
39 B3 Forebank Rd.
39 B3 Forebank St.
   Forebank Rd.
38 B1 Forest Park Pl.
38 B1 Forest Park Rd.
38 B2 Forester St.
39 A4 Forfar Rd.
39 B3 Foundry La.
38 A2 Fraser St.
38 A1 Fullarton St.
38 B1 Fyfe St.

G
38 B1 Gardners La.
39 B3 Gellatly St.
39 A3 George St., Dun.
39 A4 Gibson Ter.
39 A3 Glamis St.
38 B1 Glenagnes Rd.
38 A1 Gordon St., Dun.
38 B1 Gowrie St.
39 B4 Graham Pl.
38 C1 Greenfield Pl.
38 B2 Guthrie St.

H
39 A4 Harriet St.
38 B1 Hawkhill
38 B1 Hawkhill Pl.
38 B2 Hawkhill W.
38 B2 High St., Dun.
38 A2 Hill Sq.
38 A2 Hill St., Dun.
39 A3 Hillbank Rd.
39 A3 Hilltown
38 B2 Hilltown Ter.
38 B1 Hop St.
39 B3 Horse Wynd
38 B2 Horsewater Wynd
38 B2 Hunter St.

I
38 A1 Inverary Ter.
38 A1 Inverlaw Pl.
38 A1 Inverlaw Steps
39 A3 Isla St.

J
39 A3 Jamaica St.
39 A3 James St.
39 A4 Janefield Pl.
38 B2 Johnston St.

K
38 A2 Keats Pl.
39 B4 Kemback St.
38 A1 Kenmore Ter.
38 A2 Kennet Wk.
38 A1 Killin Av.
39 A3 Kincaldrum Pl.
39 B3 King St., Dun.
38 A2 Kinghorne Rd.
38 A1 Kinghorne Ter.
38 A2 Kinloch St.
38 A2 Kinloch Ter.
   Stirling Av.
38 A2 Kinnaird St.

39 B3 Kirk La.

L
39 B3 Ladywell Av.
39 A3 Laing Pl.
   Laing St.
39 A3 Laing St.
39 A3 Lambs La.
39 A4 Langlands St.
38 B1 Larch St.
38 B2 Laurel Bank
38 A1 Law Cres.
38 A2 Law Rd.
38 A2 Law St.
38 B1 Lawrence St., Dun.
38 A1 Lawside Av.
38 A1 Lawside Rd.
38 A1 Lawside Ter.
38 A2 Lawson Pl.
38 A2 Leng St.
39 B4 Lilybank Rd.
39 B4 Lilybank Ter.
38 A1 Lochee Rd.
38 B1 Lower Pleasance
39 A4 Lynnewood Pl.
39 B3 Lyon St.
38 B1 Lytton St.

M
38 A2 Macaulay St.
39 A4 Madeira St.
38 C1 Magdalen Pl.
39 A3 Main St.
39 A4 Mains Loan
39 A3 Mains Rd.
39 A4 Maitland St.
39 A4 Malcolm St.
38 B2 Malcolms Penn
39 C3 Marine Par.
39 B4 Market St.
38 B2 Marketgait
39 B3 Martingdale Gdns.
   Victoria Rd.
39 B3 Mary Slessor Sq.
39 B3 Maryann La.
39 A4 Maryfield Ter.
38 B2 McDonald St.
39 A4 McGill St.
38 C1 McGonall Sq.
   Patons La.
38 A2 McKinnon St.
39 B3 Meadow La.
38 B2 Meadowside
39 A4 Melrose Ter.
39 B4 Melville La.
39 A3 Mid Rd.
38 B2 Mid St.
38 B1 Mid Wynd
39 B3 Middle St.
38 B1 Millers Wynd
38 B1 Miln St.
38 B1 Milnbank Rd.
38 B1 Milnes East Wynd
38 A2 Minard Cres.
38 A1 Mitchell St.
39 A4 Molison St.
39 B4 Morgan St.
38 A2 Mortimer St.
39 B3 Murraygate

N
39 A3 Neish St.
39 A3 Nelson St.

38 C2 Nethergate
38 B2 Nicoll St.
39 A3 North Ellen St.
39 A3 North Isla St.
38 B2 North Lindsay St.
38 A2 North Somerville Pl.
38 A2 North St.
38 B2 North Tay St.
39 A3 North Wellington St
39 A3 North William St.

O
39 A3 Ogilvie St.
38 A2 Ogilvies Rd.
   Constitution St.
38 B1 Old Hawkhill
38 B2 Overgate La.

P
38 B2 Panmure St., Dun.
38 A2 Panmure Ter., Dun.
38 B2 Paradise Rd.
39 A4 Park Av., Dun.
38 A2 Park Pl., Dun.
38 B1 Park St.
38 B2 Park Wynd
38 B2 Parker St.
38 C1 Patons La.
38 B1 Peddie St.
39 B4 Peep O'day La.
38 B1 Pennycook La.
39 B3 Peter St.
38 A1 Pitfour St.
39 A4 Pitkerro Rd.
38 B1 Pole St.
38 B1 Polepark Rd.
39 B3 Princes St.
38 B2 Prospect Pl.

Q
39 B3 Queen St., Dun.

R
39 B4 Raglan St.
38 A1 Rankine St.
38 B2 Rattray St.
38 B2 Reform St.
38 A2 Reid St.
38 C1 Riverside App.
39 B4 Robertson St.
39 B4 Roodyards Rd.
38 C1 Roseangle
38 A2 Rosebank Pl.
38 A2 Rosebank Rd.
38 A2 Rosebank St.
38 A1 Rosebery St.
38 B1 Rosefield St.
38 A2 Russell Pl.
38 B1 Ryehill La.

S
39 B3 St. Andrews St.
38 B2 St. Davids La.
   North Tay St.
38 A1 St. Mary Pl.
38 A1 St. Mary St.
39 B4 St. Matthews La.
38 B1 St. Peter St.
39 B3 St. Roques La.
39 A3 St. Salvador St.
38 C2 Seabraes La.

38 C1 Seafield La.
38 C1 Seafield Rd., Dun.
39 B3 Seagate
38 B2 Session St.
39 A4 Shamrock St.
38 A2 Shelley Gdns.
39 A3 Sibbald St.
38 B2 Smalls La.
38 B2 Smalls Wynd
38 B2 Smellies La.
38 B2 Soap Works La.
38 A2 Somerville Pl.
39 B4 South Baffin St.
39 B3 South George St.
38 B2 South Tay St.
38 B2 South Ward Rd.
39 B3 South Wellington St.

38 C1 Springfield
39 B4 Springhill
39 B4 Springhill Gdns.
38 C1 Step Row
38 A2 Stirling Av.
38 A2 Stirling St.
38 A2 Stirling Ter.
Stirling Av.
39 A4 Stobswell Rd.
39 A3 Strathmore St., Dun.
39 B3 Sugar House Wynd

T
38 B1 Taits La.
39 A3 Tannadice St.
38 C2 Tay Sq.

38 C1 Tayfield Pl.
Patons La.
38 C1 Taylors La.
38 B2 Temple La.
39 A3 Thistle St.
38 C1 Thompson St.
39 B4 Thornbank Pk.
39 B4 Thornbank St.
39 B3 Trades La.
38 A1 Tullideph Pl.
38 A1 Tullideph St.

U
38 C1 Union Pl.
38 C2 Union St., Dun.
38 B2 Union Ter.
38 A2 Upper Constitution St.

38 B1 Ure St.
38 B1 Urquhart St.

V
39 B3 Victoria Rd., Dun.
39 B3 Victoria St.

W
39 B4 Wallace St.
39 A4 Walrond St.
38 B1 Walton St.
38 B2 Ward Rd.
39 B4 Watson St.
39 B3 Weavers Yd.
38 B2 West Bell St.
38 B2 West Hendersons Wynd

38 B2 West Port
38 A2 West Somerville Pl.
39 B3 West Whale La.
38 B1 West Wynd
38 C1 Westfield Av.
38 C1 Westfield La.
38 C1 Westfield Pl.
38 C2 Whitehall Cres.
38 B2 Whitehall St.
39 A4 Whortley Pl.
38 B1 Wilkies La.
39 A3 William St.
38 B2 Willison St.
38 A2 Wishart St.
Stirling Av.
39 A3 Wolseley St.

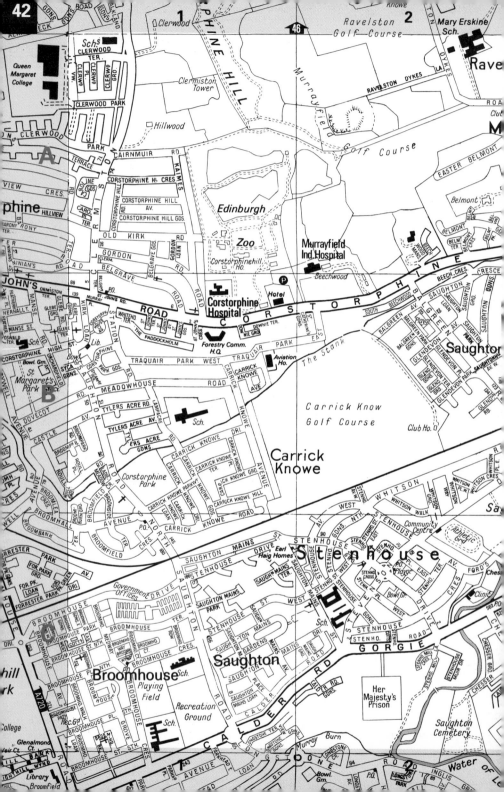

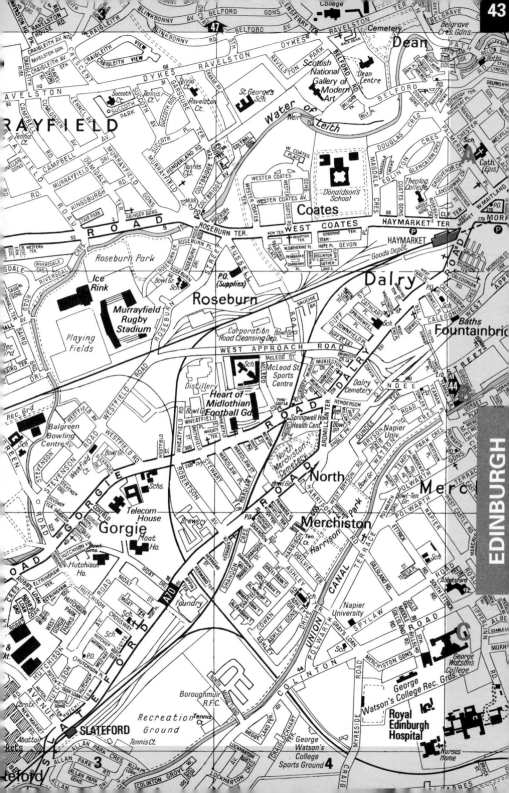

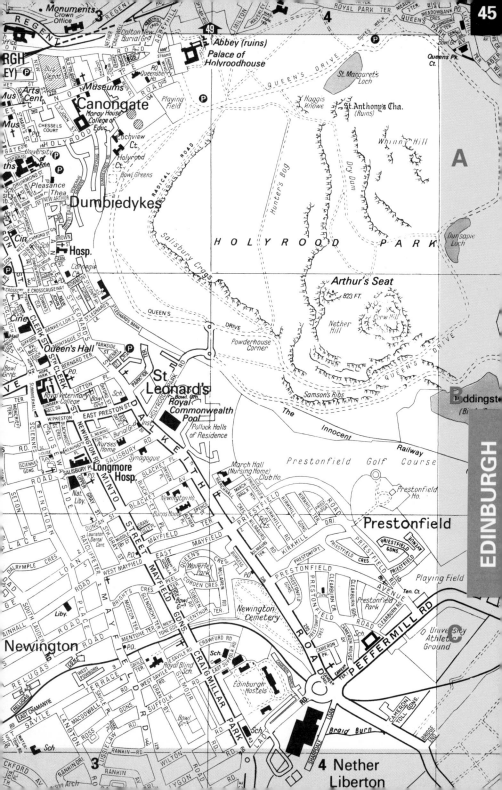

EDINBURGH

Map labels

Monuments
Crown Office
REGENT
ROYAL PARK TER.
Queen's Cres
MEADOWBANK
Queen's Walk

RGH
EY
Bus Depot
Calton Burial Grd

Abbey (ruins)
Palace of Holyroodhouse

Queen's Pk. Ct.
Queen's Drive
St Margaret's Loch
Haggis Knowe
St. Anthony's Cha. (Ruins)

Museums
Canongate
Moray House College of Educ.
Chessels Court
Lochview Ct.
Playing Field

University of Edin.
Holyrood Ct.
Bowl Greens

Whinny Hill
A

Pleasance Thea.
New Arthur
Dumbiedykes

RADICAL ROAD

Hunter's Bog
Dry Dam
Dunsapie Loch

Hosp.
Carnegie
Salisbury Crags
HOLYROOD PARK

Cine
Arthur's Seat
823 FT.
Crow Hill
Nether Hill

Queen's Hall
PARKSIDE
QUEEN'S DRIVE
Powderhouse Corner
Samson's Ribs

St Leonard's
Royal Veterinary College
Royal Commonwealth Pool
Pollock Halls of Residence
The Innocent
Railway

B
Duddingston

March Hall (Nursing Home)
Club Ho.
Prestonfield Golf Course
Prestonfield Ho.

Longmore Hosp.
Synagogue
Nat. Liby.
Burns Home
Newington Ho.

Prestonfield
PRIESTFIELD GDNS.
PRIESTFIELD
Prestonfield Park
Playing Field

Waverley Park
Newington Cemetery
PEFFERMILL RD.
University Athletic Ground
C

Newington
Libry.
Royal Blind Sch.
Edinburgh Hostels
CRAIGMILLAR PARK
CAMERON HOUSE

Bowl Grn
Braid Burn
CAMERON TOLL GDNS.

3
4 Nether Liberton
49
4

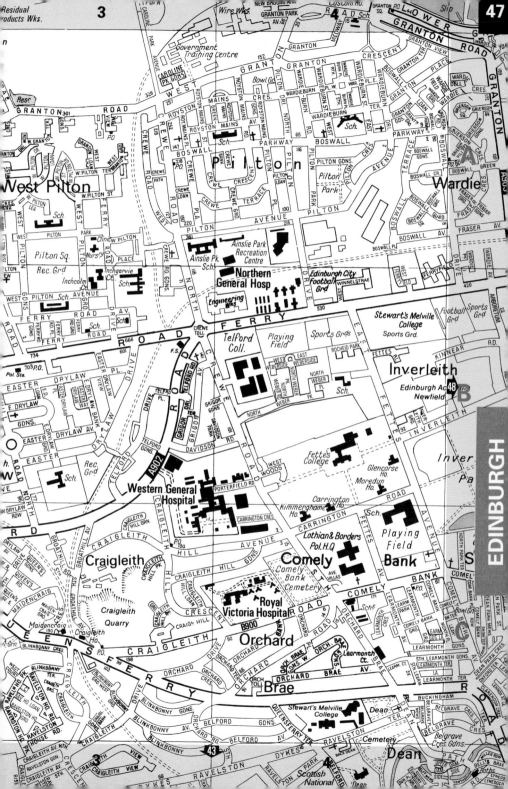

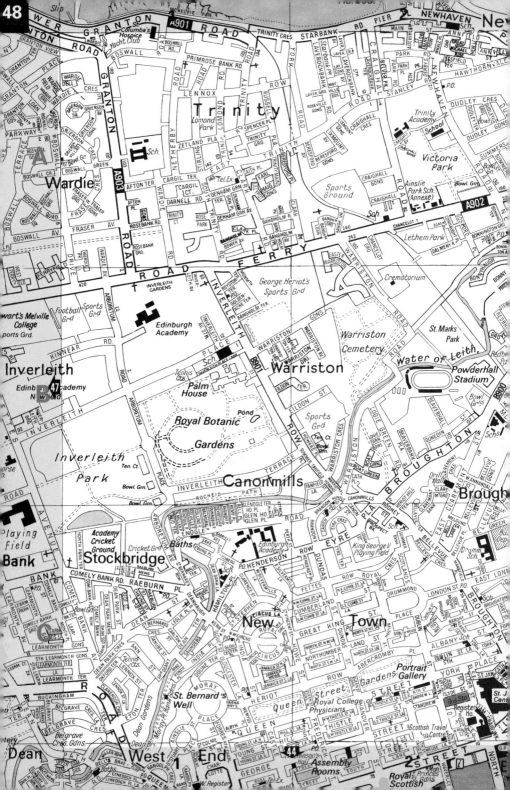

INDEX TO STREET NAMES

A

49 C3 Abbeyhill Cres.
49 C4 Abbey La.
49 C3 Abbey Mt.
45 A3 Abbey Strand
49 C3 Abbey St.
44 C1 Abbotsford Ct.
44 C1 Abbotsford Cres.
44 C1 Abbotsford Pk.
48 C2 Abercromby Pl.
43 A3 Abinger Gdns.
49 B4 Academy St.
44 B1 Admiral Ter.
43 A2 Admiralty St.
48 A1 Afton Pl.
48 A1 Afton Ter.
48 A2 Agnew Ter.
48 C1 Ainslie Pl.
48 C2 Airlie Pl.
   Brandon St.
42 A2 Aitkenhill
48 C2 Albany La.
48 C2 Albany St.
49 C3 Albert Pl.
49 A4 Albert Rd.
49 C3 Albert St.
44 C1 Albert Ter.
49 C4 Albion Pl.
49 C4 Albion Rd.
49 C4 Albion Ter.
48 C1 Albyn Pl.
43 C4 Alderbank Gdns.
   Alderbank Ter.
43 C4 Alderbank Pl.
   Alderbank Ter.
43 C4 Alderbank Ter.
43 B3 Alexander Dr.
45 C3 Alfred Pl.
43 C3 Allan Park Cres.
43 C4 Almondbank Ter.
44 B1 Alvanley Ter.
   Whitehouse Loan
49 C4 Alva Pl.
44 A1 Alva St.
49 B3 Anderson Pl.
43 B4 Angle Park Ter.
49 C3 Annandale St. La.
48 A2 Annandale St.
48 A3 Annfield
48 A2 Annfield St.
48 C1 Ann St.
49 C3 Antigua St.
42 B1 Anworth Vill.
   Saughton Rd. N.
43 C3 Appin Ter.
48 C1 Arboretum Av.
48 C1 Arboretum Rd.
44 A2 Archibald Pl.
44 B2 Arden St.
43 B4 Ardmillan Pl.
43 B4 Ardmillan Ter.
43 B4 Ardmillan Terrace La.
   Ardmillan Ter.
44 B2 Argyle Park Ter.
43 B4 Argyle Pl.
49 A3 Argyle St.
44 A1 Argyll Ter.
   Dalry Pl.
45 A3 Arthur Pl.
   Arthur St.
49 B3 Arthur St.
45 A3 Arthur St.
44 C2 Ashfield
43 C4 Ashley Dr.
43 C4 Ashley Gdns.
43 C4 Ashley Gro.
49 B3 Ashley Pl.
43 C4 Ashley Ter.
49 B4 Ashville Ter.
49 A4 Assembly St.
44 A1 Atholl Cres.
44 A1 Atholl Pl.
   West Maitland St.
44 A1 Atholl Ter.
   Dalry Pl.
48 A2 Auchinleck Ct.
48 C1 Avondale Pl.

B

43 A4 Back Dean
43 B3 Baird Av.
43 B3 Baird Dr.
43 B3 Baird Gdns.
43 B3 Baird Gro.
43 B3 Baird Ter.
48 C1 Bakers Pl.
   Kerr St.
43 A4 Balbirnie Pl.
49 B3 Balfour Pl.
49 B3 Balfour St.
42 B2 Balgreen Av.
42 B2 Balgreen Gdns.
42 B2 Balgreen Pk.
42 B2 Balgreen Rd.
49 A3 Ballantyne Lane
   Ballantyne Rd.
49 A3 Ballantyne Pl.
   Ballantyne Rd.
49 A3 Ballantyne Rd.
48 C1 Balmoral Pl.
49 A4 Baltic St.
48 A1 Bangholm Av.
48 A1 Bangholm Bower Av.
48 A2 Bangholm Gro.
48 A2 Bangholm Loan
48 A1 Bangholm Pk.
48 A1 Bangholm Pl.
48 A1 Bangholm Ter.
48 A2 Bangholm Vw.
48 A2 Bangholm Vill.
   Ferry Rd.
49 A3 Bangor Rd.
44 A2 Bank St.
44 B1 Barclay Pl.
   Bruntsfield Pl.
44 B1 Barclay Ter.
46 B1 Barnton Av. E.
46 B1 Barnton Av. S.
46 B1 Barnton Gdns.
46 B1 Barnton Loan
46 B1 Barnton Pk.
48 C2 Barony Pl.
49 A3 Barony St.
49 A3 Bathfield Rd.
44 A4 Bath Rd.
45 A3 Baxters Bldgs.
   Holyrood Rd.
49 C3 Baxters Pl.
   Leith Wk.
44 C2 Beaufort Rd.
48 B2 Beaverbank Pl.
48 B2 Beaverhall Rd.
48 C1 Bedford Ct.
48 C1 Bedford St.
42 A2 Beechmount Cres.
49 B4 Beechwood Ter.
47 C4 Belford Av.
43 A4 Belford Bridge
   Belford Rd.
47 C4 Belford Gdns.
43 A4 Belford Mews
43 A4 Belford Pk.
43 A4 Belford Pl.
43 A4 Belford Rd.
43 A4 Belford Ter.
   Belford Rd.
47 C4 Belgrave Cres.
48 C1 Belgrave Crescent La.
42 A1 Belgrave Gdns.
47 C4 Belgrave Mews
47 C4 Belgrave Pl.
42 A1 Belgrave Rd.
42 B1 Belgrave Ter.
48 C2 Bellevue
48 C2 Bellevue Cres.
48 B2 Bellevue Gdns.
48 C2 Bellevue La.
48 C2 Bellevue Gro.
48 C2 Bellevue Pl.
48 C2 Bellevue Rd.
48 C2 Bellevue St.
48 C2 Bellevue Ter.
48 C1 Bell Pl.
44 B1 Bells Brae
44 A2 Bells Wynd
   High St.

42 A2 Belmont Av.
42 A2 Belmont Cres.
42 A2 Belmont Gdns.
42 A2 Belmont Pk.
42 A2 Belmont Ter.
42 A2 Belmont Vw.
48 A2 Belvedere Pk.
48 A2 Beresford Av.
48 A2 Beresford Gdns.
48 A1 Beresford Pl.
48 A2 Beresford Ter.
   Trinity Rd.
49 A4 Bernard St.
45 B3 Bernard Ter.
46 A2 Birnies Ct.
45 B3 Blacket Av.
45 B3 Blacket Pl.
45 C3 Blackford Bank
44 C2 Blackford Av.
44 C2 Blackford House
44 C2 Blackford Rd.
45 A3 Blackfriars St.
49 B4 Blackie Rd.
45 B3 Blackwood Cres.
44 A2 Blair St.
44 C1 Blantyre Ter.
49 C3 Blenheim Pl.
47 C3 Blinkbonny Av.
47 C3 Blinkbonny Gdns.
47 C3 Blinkbonny Gro.
47 C3 Blinkbonny Gro. W.
43 A3 Blinkbonny Rd.
47 C3 Blinkbonny Ter.
48 B2 Boat Grn.
48 A2 Bonar Pl.
   Ferry Rd.
48 A2 Bonnington Av.
48 A2 Bonnington Gro.
49 B3 Bonnington Rd.
49 B3 Bonnington Road La.
48 A2 Bonnington Ter.
45 B3 Boroughloch Bldgs.
   Boroughloch Sq.
45 B3 Boroughloch La.
45 B3 Boroughloch Sq.
   Boroughloch La.
44 A2 Borthwick Clo.
   High St.
43 A4 Borthwick Pl.
47 A4 Boswall Av.
47 A4 Boswall Cres.
47 A4 Boswall Dr.
47 A4 Boswall Gdns.
48 A1 Boswall Grn.
47 A4 Boswall Gro.
47 A4 Boswall Loan
47 A4 Boswall Parkway
47 A4 Boswall Pl.
47 A4 Boswall Quadrant
48 A1 Boswall Rd.
47 A4 Boswall Sq.
45 B3 Bothwell St.
48 B1 Bowhill Ter.
   Ferry Rd.
49 A4 Bowies Clo.
   Queen St.
49 A3 Bowling Green St.
49 A3 Bowling Green St. W.
   Bowling Green St.
45 B3 Bowmont Pl.
45 A3 Boyds Entry
   St. Marys St.
44 B1 Brandfield St.
48 C2 Brandon St.
48 C2 Brandon Ter.
49 C3 Brand Pl.
   Abbeyhill
49 B3 Breadalbane St.
44 A1 Breadalbane Ter.
   Dalry Pl.
44 A1 Bread St.
49 A3 Brewery La.
   Great Junction St.
43 C4 Briarbank Ter.
49 A3 Brickwork Clo.
   Giles St.
45 C4 Bridge End

48 C1 Bridge Pl.
   Glenogle Rd.
45 A3 Briery Bauks
44 A2 Brighton St.
45 C3 Brights Cres.
44 A1 Bright Ter.
   Dairy Pl.
44 A2 Bristo Pl.
44 A2 Bristo Port
49 A4 Broad Wynd
42 C1 Broomburn Gro.
42 C1 Broomfield Cres.
42 C1 Broomhouse Bank
42 C1 Broomhouse Cotts.
42 C1 Broomhouse Cotts. E.
42 C1 Broomhouse Cres.
42 C1 Broomhouse Gdns. E.
42 C1 Broomhouse Gro.
42 C1 Broomhouse Loan
42 C1 Broomhouse Medway
42 C1 Broomhouse Pl. S.
42 C1 Broomhouse Row
42 C1 Broomhouse Sq.
42 C1 Broomhouse Ter.
42 C1 Broomhouse Wk.
42 C1 Broomhouse Way
42 C1 Broomhouse Wynd
42 B1 Broompark Rd.
42 B1 Broomside Pl.
44 B1 Brougham Pl.
44 B1 Brougham St.
48 C2 Broughton Market
48 C2 Broughton Pl.
48 C2 Broughton Pl. E.
   Broughton Pl.
48 B2 Broughton Rd.
48 C2 Broughton Street La.
48 C2 Broughton St.
45 A3 Browns Clo.
44 A2 Browns Pl.
   Vennel
45 A3 Brown St.
49 C3 Brunswick Pl.
49 C3 Brunswick Rd.
49 C3 Brunswick St.
49 C3 Brunton Gdns.
   Montgomery St.
49 C3 Brunton Pl.
49 C3 Brunton Ter.
44 B1 Bruntsfield Av.
44 B1 Bruntsfield Cres.
44 B1 Bruntsfield Gdns.
44 B1 Bruntsfield Pl.
44 B1 Bruntsfield Ter.
43 B4 Bryson Rd.
44 B2 Buccleuch Pl.
45 B3 Buccleuch St.
45 B3 Buccleuch Ter.
49 B3 Buchanan St.
47 C4 Buckingham Ter.
44 A4 Burgess St.
45 C4 Burgess Ter.
49 A3 Burlington St.
49 B4 Burns St.

C

49 A3 Cables Wynd
49 A3 Cables Wynd Ho.
49 A4 Cadiz St.
49 C4 Cadzow Pl.
42 A1 Cairngorm Ho.
42 A1 Cairnmuir Rd.
42 A1 Caithness Pl.
42 C2 Calder Road Gdns.
43 B4 Caledonian Cres.
43 B4 Caledonian Pl.
44 B1 Caledonian Rd.
49 C3 Calton Hill
45 A3 Calton Rd.
49 B3 Cambridge Av.
49 B3 Cambridge Gdns.
44 A1 Cambridge Street La.
44 A1 Cambridge St.
45 C4 Cameron Cres.

45 C4 Cameron House Av.
45 C4 Cameron Pk.
45 C4 Cameron Ter.
45 C4 Cameron Toll Gdns.
43 A3 Campbell Av.
43 A3 Campbell Rd.
45 A3 Campbells Clo.
49 C4 Cambusnethan St.
44 C1 Canaan La.
44 A2 Candlemaker Row
44 A1 Canning Street La.
44 A1 Canning St.
48 C2 Cannon La.
49 A3 Cannon Wynd
45 A3 Canongate
48 B2 Canonmills
48 C2 Canon St.
43 A4 Carberry Pl.
46 C2 Carfrae Gdns.
46 C2 Carfrae Gro.
46 C2 Carfrae Pk.
46 C2 Carfrae Rd.
48 A1 Cargil Ct.
48 A1 Cargil Ter.
49 C3 Carlton St.
49 C3 Carlton Ter.
49 C4 Carlyle Pl.
45 A3 Carnegie Ct.
45 A3 Carnegie St.
42 A1 Caroline Gdns.
47 A3 Caroline Park Av.
42 A1 Caroline Pl.
49 A4 Carpet La.
42 B1 Carrick Knowe Av.
42 B1 Carrick Knowe Dr.
42 B1 Carrick Knowe Gdns.
42 B1 Carrick Knowe Gro.
42 B1 Carrick Knowe Hill
42 B1 Carrick Knowe Loan
42 B1 Carrick Knowe Parkway
42 B1 Carrick Knowe Pl.
42 C1 Carrick Knowe Rd.
42 B1 Carrick Knowe Ter.
47 C4 Carrington Rd.
44 A2 Carrubbers Clo.
   High St.
49 B3 Casselbank St.
49 B3 Cassels La.
44 A2 Castle Esplanade
44 A2 Castlehill
44 A1 Castle St.
44 A1 Castle Ter.
44 A2 Castle Wynd N.
   Johnston Ter.
44 A2 Castle Wynd S.
   Johnston Ter.
43 B4 Cathcart Pl.
48 C2 Cathedral La.
45 B3 Causewayside
44 B1 Chalmers Bldgs.
   Fountainbridge
45 A3 Chalmers Clo.
44 B2 Chalmers Cres.
44 B2 Chalmers St.
44 C1 Chamberlain Rd.
44 A2 Chambers St.
48 A2 Chancelot Cres.
   Ferry Rd.
48 A2 Chancelot Gro.
48 A2 Chancelot Ter.
49 A4 Chapel La.
45 B3 Chapel St.
44 A2 Charlesfield
   Bristo Sq.
44 A2 Charles Street La.
44 A2 Charles St.
   George Sq.
44 A1 Charlotte La.
44 A1 Charlotte Sq.
49 C3 Charlton Terrace La.
44 C2 Charterhall Gro.
42 C2 Chesser Av.
43 C3 Chesser Cres.
42 C2 Chesser Gdns.
42 C2 Chesser Gro.
42 C2 Chesser Loan
45 A3 Chessels
44 A1 Chester St.
48 C1 Cheyne St.

44 C1 Church Hill
44 C1 Churchill Dri.
44 C1 Church Hill Pl.
48 C1 Circus Gdns.
48 C1 Circus La.
49 A3 Citadel Pl.
  Commercial St.
48 C1 Citadel St.
49 C4 Clapperton Pl.
  Lower London Rd.
49 B4 Clarebank Cres.
48 C2 Claremont Bank
48 B2 Claremont Cres.
49 B4 Claremont Gdns.
48 B2 Claremont Gro.
49 B4 Claremont Pk.
48 B4 Claremont Rd.
48 C1 Clarence St.
48 C1 Clarendon Cres.
48 A2 Clark Av.
48 A1 Clark Pl.
48 A1 Clark St.
45 C4 Clearburn Cres.
45 C4 Clearburn Gdns.
45 C4 Clearburn Rd.
45 B3 Clerk St.
46 C1 Clermiston Hill
42 A1 Clermiston Rd.
46 C1 Clermiston Rd. N.
42 A1 Clermiston Ter.
46 C1 Clermiston Vw.
42 A1 Clerwood Gro.
42 A1 Clerwood Pl.
42 A1 Clerwood Ter.
42 A1 Clerwood Vw.
48 A2 Clifton Ter.
44 C1 Clinton Rd.
49 C4 Clockmill La.
44 C2 Cluny Pl.
48 C2 Clyde St.
49 A3 Coal Hill
44 A1 Coates Cres.
43 A4 Coates Gdns.
44 A1 Coates Pl.
  West Maitland St.
49 A4 Coatfield La.
45 C3 Cobden Cres.
45 C3 Cobden Rd.
44 A1 Cobden Ter.
  Dalry Rd.
49 A3 Coburg St.
49 B4 Cochrane Pl.
48 C2 Cochran Pl.
  East London St.
48 C2 Cochran Ter.
44 A2 Cockburn St.
45 A3 Coinyie-House Clo.
  Blackfriars St
44 C1 Colinton Rd.
43 C4 Colinton Rd.
44 A2 College Wynd
  Cowgate
43 A3 Collins Pl.
43 A3 Coltbridge Av.
43 A4 Coltbridge Gdns.
43 A3 Coltbridge Ter.
44 A4 Coltbridge Vale
46 C2 Columba Av.
46 C2 Columba Rd.
48 C1 Colville Pl.
47 C4 Comely Bank
48 C1 Comely Bank Av.
47 C4 Comely Bank Gro.
48 C1 Comely Bank Pl.
48 C1 Comely Bank Place
  Mews
  Comely Bank Pl.
48 C1 Comely Bank Rd.
48 C1 Comely Bank Row
47 C4 Comely Bank St.
48 C1 Comely Bank Ter.
49 C4 Comely Green Cres.
49 C4 Comely Green Pl.
48 A2 Commercial St.
49 A4 Constitution Pl.
  Tower Street La.
49 A4 Constitution St.
46 B2 Corbiehill Av.

46 B1 Corbiehill Cres.
46 B2 Corbiehill Gdns.
46 B2 Corbiehill Gro.
46 B2 Corbiehill Pk.
46 B1 Corbiehill Pl.
46 B1 Corbiehill Rd.
46 B1 Corbiehill Ter.
43 C3 Corn Exchange
  Bldgs.
  New Market Rd.
49 B4 Cornhill Ter.
48 C2 Cornwallis Pl.
  Bellevue Cres.
44 A1 Cornwall St.
44 B2 Coronation Wk.
42 A1 Corstorphine Hill
  Av.
42 A1 Corstorphine Hill
  Cres.
42 A1 Corstorphine Hill
  Gdns.
42 A1 Corstorphine Hill
  Rd.
42 B1 Corstorphine Ho.
  Av.
42 B1 Corstorphine Ho.
  Ter.
42 B1 Corstorphine Park
  Gdns.
42 B1 Corstorphine Rd.
49 A3 Corunna Pl.
49 A3 Couper St.
43 C4 Cowan Rd.
45 B3 Cowans Clo.
44 A2 Cowgate
44 A2 Cowgatehead
46 C1 Craigcrook Av.
46 C2 Craigcrook Gro.
46 C2 Craigcrook Pk.
46 C2 Craigcrook Pl.
  Craigcrook Av.
46 C1 Craigcrook Rd.
46 C2 Craigcrook Sq.
48 A2 Craighall Av.
48 A2 Craighall Bank
  Craighall Av.
48 A2 Craighall Cres.
48 A2 Craighall Gdns.
48 A2 Craighall Rd.
48 A2 Craighall Ter.
43 A3 Craigleith Av. N.
43 A3 Craigleith Av. S.
47 C3 Craigleith Bank
47 C3 Craigleith Cres.
47 C3 Craigleith Dr.
47 C3 Craigleith Gdns.
47 C3 Craigleith Gro.
47 C3 Craigleith Hill
47 C3 Craigleith Hill Av.
47 C3 Craigleith Hill Cres.
47 C3 Craigleith Hill
  Gdns.
47 C3 Craigleith Hill Grn.
47 C3 Craigleith Hill Gro.
47 C3 Craigleith Hill Loan
47 C3 Craigleith Hill Pk.
47 C3 Craigleith Hill Row
47 C3 Craigleith House
43 A3 Craigleith Ri.
47 C3 Craigleith Rd.
43 A3 Craigleith Vw.
43 C4 Craiglockhart Ter.
45 C4 Craigmillar Pk.
45 A3 Cranston St.
43 A3 Crarae Av.
49 C4 Crawford Bri.
45 C4 Crawfurd Rd.
43 B3 Crescent, The,
  Gorgie Rd.
44 A4 Crewe Bank
47 A4 Crewe Cres.
47 A4 Crewe Gro.
47 A3 Crewe Loan
47 A4 Crewe Path
47 A3 Crewe Pl.
47 A3 Crewe Road Gdns.
47 A3 Crewe Rd. N.
47 B4 Crewe Rd. S.
47 A3 Crewe Rd. W.
47 A4 Crewe Ter.

47 B3 Crewe Toll
44 A2 Crichton St.
49 B3 Crighton Pl.
49 C3 Croall Pl.
49 C3 Croft-an-righ
49 A3 Cromwell Pl.
  Commercial St.
49 B3 Crown Pl.
49 B3 Crown St.
48 C2 Cumberland St.
45 C3 Cumin Pl.
43 A3 Cumlodden Av.
49 B3 Cunningham Pl.
  Jane St.

D
43 C4 Daisy Ter.
  Merchiston Gro.
49 C4 Dalgety Av.
49 C4 Dalgety Rd.
49 C4 Dalgety St.
45 B3 Dalkeith Rd.
49 B3 Dalmeny Rd.
49 B3 Dalmeny St.
45 C3 Dalrymple Cres.
44 A1 Dalry Pl.
43 B4 Dalry Rd.
49 C4 Dalziel Pl.
  London Rd.
43 A4 Damside
48 C1 Danube St.
48 C1 Darlings Bldgs.
  Saunders St.
48 C1 Darnaway St.
48 A1 Darnell Rd.
46 B2 Davidson Gdns.
47 B3 Davidson Pk.
47 B3 Davidson Rd.
45 A3 Davie St.
48 C1 Dean Bank La.
48 C1 Dean Bank Ter.
  West Claremont St.
48 C1 Deanhaugh St.
48 C1 Dean Park Cres.
48 C1 Dean Park Mews
48 C1 Dean Park St.
47 C4 Dean Path
48 C1 Dean
48 C1 Dean Ter.
43 C3 Delhaig
48 A1 Denham Green Av.
48 A1 Denham Green Pl.
48 A1 Denham Green
  Ter.
48 A2 Derby St.
43 A4 Devon Pl.
44 A1 Dewar La.
44 A1 Dewar Pl.
44 C2 Dick Pl.
44 A2 Dicksons Clo.
  High St.
44 A2 Dicksons Ct.
  Bristo St.
43 B3 Dickson St.
44 A1 Distillery La.
  Dalry Rd.
49 A3 Dock Pl.
49 A3 Dock St.
44 B1 Dorset Pl.
43 A4 Douglas Cres.
43 A4 Douglas Gdns.
43 A4 Douglas Gardens
  Mews
  Belford Rd.
44 A1 Douglas Ter.
  Dalry Pl.
48 C1 Doune Ter.
43 B4 Downfield Pl.
42 B1 Downie Gro.
42 B1 Downie Ter.
49 C4 Dr. Begg
44 B1 Drumdryan St.
49 B3 Drummond Pl.
45 A3 Drummond St.
49 C4 Drum Park Yard
  Albion Rd.
44 A1 Drumsheugh Gdns.
44 A1 Drumsheugh Pl.
  Queensferry St.

49 C4 Drum Ter.
49 B3 Dryden Gdns.
45 B3 Dryden Pl.
49 B3 Dryden St.
49 B3 Dryden Ter.
47 C3 Drylaw Av.
46 C2 Drylaw Cres.
46 B2 Drylaw Gdns.
46 C2 Drylaw Grn.
46 C2 Drylaw Gro.
46 B2 Drylaw House
  Gdns.
46 B2 Drylaw House
  Paddock
48 C2 Dublin Meuse
48 C2 Dublin Street La.
  N.
  Dublin St.
48 C2 Dublin St.
48 A2 Dudley Av.
49 A3 Dudley Av. S.
48 A2 Dudley Bank
48 A2 Dudley Cres.
48 A2 Dudley Gdns.
48 A2 Dudley Gro.
48 A2 Dudley Ter.
43 B4 Duff Street La.
43 B4 Duff St.
48 B4 Duke Pl.
48 C2 Duke Street La.
48 B4 Duke St.
49 C4 Dukes Wk.
45 A3 Dumbiedykes Rd.
44 C2 Dun-Ard Gdns.
44 B1 Dunbar St.
49 B4 Duncan Pl.
45 C3 Duncan St.
48 C2 Dundas St.
44 B1 Dundee Pl.
43 B4 Dundee St.
43 B4 Dundee Ter.
48 B2 Dundonald St.
44 B2 Dunedin St.
44 A2 Dunlops Ct.
  Grassmarket
48 C1 Dunrobin Pl.

E
44 A1 Earl Grey St.
48 A1 Earl Haig Gdns.
49 C4 Earlston Pl.
  London Rd.
45 A3 East Adam St.
46 B1 East Barnton Gdns.
48 C2 East Broughton Pl.
  Broughton Pl.
44 B1 East Castle Rd.
45 C3 East Chamanyie
48 C2 East Claremont St.
47 C3 East Ct.
49 A3 East Cromwell St.
45 B3 East
  Crosscauseway
42 A2 Easter Belmont Rd.
47 B3 Easter Drylaw Av.
47 B3 Easter Drylaw
  Bank
47 B3 Easter Drylaw Dr.
47 B3 Easter Drylaw
  Gdns.
47 B3 Easter Drylaw Gro.
47 B3 Easter Drylaw
  Loan
47 B3 Easter Drylaw Pl.
47 B3 Easter Drylaw Vw.
47 B3 Easter Drylaw Way
49 B4 Easter Hermitage
  Restalrig Rd.
46 B1 Easter Park Dr.
49 C3 Easter Rd.
47 B4 East Fettes Av.
49 B4 East Hermitage Pl.
48 A1 East Lillypot
48 C2 East London St.
45 A3 East Market St.
45 C3 East Mayfield
49 C3 East Montgomery
  Pl.
45 B3 East Newington Pl.

49 C3 East Norton Pl.
  London Rd.
45 B3 East Preston St.
49 B4 East Restalrig Ter.
48 C2 East St. James St.
  South St. James
  St.
45 C3 East Savile Rd.
48 C1 East Silvermills La.
45 C4 East Suffolk Rd.
48 A1 East Trinity Rd.
47 B4 East Weberside
44 C1 Eden La.
44 C1 Eden Ter.
  Morningside Rd.
49 C4 Edina Pl.
49 C3 Edina St.
43 A4 Eglinton Cres.
44 C2 Egypt Mews
48 B2 Eildon St.
48 B1 Eildon Ter.
49 A4 Elbe St.
48 C2 Elder St.
48 C2 Elder St. E.
43 A4 Elgin Pl.
49 C3 Elgin St. N.
49 C3 Elgin St. S.
49 C3 Elgin Ter.
49 B3 Elizafield
42 A2 Ellersly Rd.
49 C3 Elliot St.
49 B4 Elm Pl.
49 C3 Elm Row
49 B4 Elmwood Ter.
43 C3 Eltringham Gdns.
43 C3 Eltringham Gro.
43 C3 Eltringham Ter.
44 A1 Erskine Pl.
  Shandwick Pl.
48 C1 Eton Ter.
48 C1 Ettrickdale Pl.
44 B1 Ettrick Gro.
43 C4 Ettrick Rd.
48 C2 Eyre Cres.
48 C2 Eyre Pl.
48 C2 Eyre Ter.

F
44 C1 Falcon Av.
44 C1 Falcon Ct.
44 C1 Falcon Gdns.
44 C1 Falcon Rd.
44 C1 Falcon Rd. W.
46 C1 Falkland Gdns.
47 A4 Ferryfield
46 B2 Ferry Rd.
48 A2 Ferry Rd.
47 B3 Ferry Road Av.
47 A3 Ferry Road Dr.
47 B3 Ferry Road Gdns.
47 B3 Ferry Road Gro.
47 B3 Ferry Road Pl.
47 B4 Fettes Ri.
48 C2 Fettes Row
42 A2 Fidra Ct.
45 C3 Findhorn Pl.
44 B2 Fingal Pl.
49 B4 Fingzies Pl.
44 A2 Fleshmarket Clo.
  High St.
44 C1 Forbes Rd.
45 B3 Forbes St.
42 C2 Fords Rd.
48 C1 Forres St.
44 A2 Forrest Hill
44 A2 Forrest Rd.
49 A3 Fort Ho.
48 C2 Forth St.
47 C3 Forthview Rd.
46 C2 Forthview Ter.
49 A3 Fort Pl.
44 B1 Fountainbridge
45 C4 Fountainhall Rd.
43 B4 Fowler Ter.
46 C1 Fox Covert Av.
46 C1 Fox Covert Gro.
49 A4 Fox St.
48 A1 Fraser Av.
48 A1 Fraser Cres.

48	A1	Fraser Gdns.
48	A1	Fraser Gro.
48	C2	Frederick St.
44	B1	Freer Street Ter.
		Freer St.
44	B1	Freer St.
		G
48	C1	Gabriels Rd.
46	B1	Garden Ter.
46	C2	Gardiner Gro.
46	C2	Gardiner Rd.
46	C2	Gardiner Ter.
44	A1	Gardners Cres.
49	C4	Gardner St.
		Lower London Rd.
43	A3	Garscube Ter.
49	C3	Gayfield Pl.
49	C3	Gayfield Place La.
49	C3	Gayfield Sq.
49	C3	Gayfield St.
44	A2	Generals Entry
		Bristo St.
44	B2	George Sq.
44	B2	George Square La.
44	A1	George St.
44	A2	George IV Bridge
45	A3	Gibbs Entry
		Simon Sq.
49	B3	Gibson St.
44	B1	Gibson Ter.
45	B3	Gifford Pk.
49	A3	Giles St.
44	B1	Gillespie Cres.
44	B1	Gillespie Pl.
		Leven St.
44	B1	Gillespie St.
		Gilmore Pl.
43	C4	Gillsland Pk.
43	C4	Gillsland Rd.
44	B1	Gilmore Pl.
44	B1	Gilmore Place La.
45	C3	Gilmour Rd.
45	A3	Gilmour St.
49	B4	Gladstone Pl.
45	B3	Gladstone Ter.
48	C1	Glanville Pl.
		Kerr St.
42	B1	Glebe Gdns.
43	A4	Glencairn Cres.
42	B2	Glendevon Av.
42	B2	Glendevon Gdns.
42	B2	Glendevon Gro.
42	B2	Glendevon Pk.
42	B2	Glendevon Pl.
42	B2	Glendevon Rd.
42	B2	Glendevon Ter.
44	A1	Glenfinlas St.
44	B1	Glengyle Ter.
44	C2	Glenisla Gdns.
43	C3	Glenlea Cotts.
48	C1	Glenogle Ho.
		Bell Pl.
48	C1	Glenogle Pl.
		Bell Pl.
48	C1	Glenogle Rd.
48	C1	Glenogle Ter.
		Bell Pl.
49	C3	Glenorchy Pl.
		Greenside Row
45	C3	Glenorchy Ter.
44	B2	Glen St.
48	C1	Gloucester La.
48	C1	Gloucester Pl.
48	C1	Gloucester Sq.
		Gloucester La.
48	C1	Gloucester St.
49	B4	Glover St.
48	B1	Goldenacre Ter.
42	A1	Gordon Loan
42	A1	Gordon Rd.
49	B4	Gordon St.
43	C3	Gorgie Cotts.
42	C2	Gorgie Rd.
48	A2	Gosford Pl.
49	A3	Graham St.
49	A3	Grampian Ho.
45	C3	Granby Rd.

45	B3	Grange Ct.
		Causewayside
44	C2	Grange Cres.
44	C2	Grange Loan
44	C2	Grange Loan Gdns.
44	B2	Grange Rd.
44	C2	Grange Ter.
47	A4	Granton Cres.
47	A4	Granton Gdns.
47	A4	Granton Gro.
47	A4	Granton Medway
47	A4	Granton Pl.
48	A1	Granton Rd.
47	A4	Granton Ter.
47	A4	Granton Vw.
45	C3	Grantully Pl.
44	B1	Granville Ter.
44	A2	Grassmarket
43	C4	Grays Loan
49	A3	Great Junction St.
48	C2	Great King St.
48	A2	Great Michael Ri.
44	A1	Great Stuart St.
44	C1	Greenhill Gdns.
44	C1	Greenhill Pk.
44	C1	Greenhill Pl.
44	B1	Greenhill Ter.
49	C3	Greenside Ct.
49	C3	Greenside La.
49	C3	Greenside Pl.
		Leith St.
49	C3	Greenside Row
48	C2	Green St.
46	B1	Green, The,
44	A2	Greyfriars Pl.
		Candlemaker Row
48	A1	Grierson Av.
48	A1	Grierson Cres.
48	A1	Grierson Gdns.
47	A4	Grierson Rd.
48	A1	Grierson Sq.
48	A1	Grierson Vill.
47	B3	Grigor Av.
47	B3	Grigor Dr.
47	B3	Grigor Gdns.
47	B3	Grigor Ter.
44	A1	Grindlay St.
44	A1	Grindlay Street Ct.
47	C3	Groathill Av.
47	C3	Groathill Gdns. E.
		Groathill Rd. S.
47	C3	Groathill Gdns. W.
		Groathill Rd. S.
47	B3	Groathill Rd. N.
47	C3	Groathill Rd. S.
43	A4	Grosvenor Cres.
43	A4	Grosvenor Gdns.
44	A1	Grosvenor St.
44	A1	Grove St.
44	A1	Grove Ter.
		Grove St.
45	A3	Gullans Clo.
		St. Marys St.
46	A2	Gunnet Ct.
44	A2	Guthrie St.
		H
49	C3	Haddington Pl.
45	A3	Haddingtons Entry
		Reids Clo.
45	B3	Haddon Ct.
		Howden St.
44	B1	Hailes St.
49	B3	Halmyre St.
49	A3	Hamburgh Pl.
49	A3	Hamilton Cres.
48	C1	Hamilton Pl.
48	A3	Hamilton St.
49	A3	Hamilton Wynd
43	A4	Hampton Pl.
		West Catherine Pl.
43	A4	Hampton Ter.
43	B4	Harden Pl.
45	B3	Hardwell Clo.
43	C4	Harrison Gdns.
43	C4	Harrison La.
43	C4	Harrison Pl.
43	B4	Harrison Rd.

44	B1	Hartington Gdns.
44	B1	Hartington Pl.
48	C2	Hart St.
44	B2	Hatton Pl.
48	C1	Haugh St.
49	B4	Hawkhill Av.
49	B4	Hawkhill Ct.
49	B4	Hawkhill Vill.
		Lochend Rd.
44	A1	Hawthornbank
44	A1	Hawthornbank La.
49	A3	Hawthornbank Pl.
49	A3	Hawthornbank Ter.
		North Fort St.
44	A1	Hawthorn Bldgs.
		Belford Rd.
44	A1	Hawthorn Ter.
		Hawthornbank La.
48	A2	Hawthornvale
44	A1	Haymarket
43	A4	Haymarket Ter.
43	C4	Hazelbank Ter.
43	A3	Henderland Rd.
49	A3	Henderson Gdns.
48	C2	Henderson Pl.
48	C1	Henderson Row
49	A3	Henderson St.
43	B4	Henderson Ter.
45	B3	Henry Pl.
45	B3	Henry St.
44	A2	Heriot Bridge
44	A2	Heriot Cross
		Heriot Bridge
48	B2	Heriot Hill Ter.
44	A2	Heriot Pl.
48	C1	Heriot Row
43	C4	Hermand Cres.
43	C3	Hermand St.
43	C3	Hermand Ter.
49	B4	Hermitage Pk.
49	B4	Hermitage Park Gro.
49	B4	Hermitage Pk. S.
		Hermitage Pk.
49	B4	Hermitage Pl.
44	A1	High Riggs
45	A3	High School Yards
44	A2	High St.
46	B1	Hillhouse Rd.
46	C1	Hillpark Av.
46	C1	Hillpark Brae
46	B1	Hillpark Ct.
46	C1	Hillpark Cres.
46	B1	Hillpark Dr.
46	C1	Hillpark Gdns.
46	C1	Hillpark Gro.
46	C2	Hillpark Loan
46	C2	Hillpark Pl.
46	C1	Hillpark Rd.
46	C1	Hillpark Vw.
46	C2	Hillpark Way
46	C2	Hillpark Wood
45	A3	Hill Pl.
48	C1	Hill Street La. N.
44	A1	Hill Street La. S.
49	C3	Hillside Cres.
49	C3	Hillside St.
45	A3	Hill Sq.
		Hill Pl.
48	C1	Hill St.
45	A3	Hillview
43	C4	Hollybank Ter.
45	B3	Holyrood Ct.
45	B3	Holyrood Park Rd.
45	A3	Holyrood Rd.
44	B1	Home St.
49	A3	Hopefield Ter.
45	B3	Hope Park Cres..
44	B2	Hope Park Sq.
		Meadow La.
45	B3	Hope Park Ter.
44	A1	Hope Street La.
44	A1	Hope St.
44	C2	Hope Ter.
49	C3	Hopetoun Cres.
49	C3	Hopetoun Crescent La.
49	B3	Hopetoun St.
44	A1	Horne Ter.
45	A3	Horse Wynd
46	B2	House O'Hill Av.

46	B2	House O'Hill Brae
46	B2	House O'Hill Cres.
46	B2	House O'Hill Gdns.
46	B2	House O'Hill Grn.
46	B2	House O'Hill Gro.
46	B2	House O'Hill Pl.
46	B2	House O'Hill Rd.
46	B2	House O'Hill Row
48	B2	Howard Pl.
48	B2	Howard St.
45	B3	Howden St.
48	C2	Howe St.
48	C1	Hugh Miller Pl.
44	A2	Hunter Sq.
48	B2	Huntly St.
43	C3	Hutchison Av.
43	C3	Hutchison Cotts.
43	C3	Hutchison Crossway
43	C3	Hutchison Gdns.
42	B1	Hutchison Gro.
43	C3	Hutchison Ho.
43	C3	Hutchison Loan
43	C3	Hutchison Medway
43	C3	Hutchison Pl.
43	C3	Hutchison Rd.
43	C3	Hutchison Ter.
43	C3	Hutchison Vw.
		I
47	B3	Inchcolm Ct.
47	B3	Inchgarvie Ct.
49	B3	Inchkeith Ct.
44	A2	India Bldgs.
		Victoria St.
48	C1	India Pl.
48	C1	India St.
49	B4	Industrial Rd.
49	A3	Industry Homes
		Industry La.
49	A3	Industry La.
45	A3	Infirmary St.
44	A2	Inglis Ct.
		West Port
48	B1	Inverleith Av.
48	B1	Inverleith Av. S.
48	B1	Inverleith Gdns.
47	B4	Inverleith Gro.
47	B4	Inverleith Pl.
48	B1	Inverleith Place La.
48	B1	Inverleith Row
48	B1	Inverleith Ter.
49	B3	Iona St.
43	C4	Ivy Ter.
		J
48	C1	Jamaica Mews
48	C1	Jamaica St. N. La.
48	C1	Jamaica St. S. La.
44	A2	James Ct.
		Lawnmarket
48	C2	James Craig Wk.
49	B3	Jameson Pl.
49	B3	James St.
49	B3	Jane St.
49	C4	Jane Ter.
44	B2	Jawbone Wk.
46	C2	Jeffrey Av.
45	A3	Jeffrey St.
48	A2	Jessfield Ter.
49	A3	John Russel Ct.
		Cromwell Pl.
49	A4	Johns La.
49	A4	Johns Pl.
44	A2	Johnston Ter.
44	C1	Jordan La.
49	B3	Junction Pl.
		K
42	A1	Kaimes Rd.
44	A2	Keir St.
46	C2	Keith Cres.
46	C2	Keith Row
		Craigcrook Rd.
46	C2	Keith Ter.
48	C1	Kemp Pl.
48	C1	Kerr St.
43	A4	Kew Ter.

44	C2	Kilgraston Ct.
44	C2	Kilgraston Rd.
45	C4	Kilmaurs Rd.
45	C4	Kilmaurs Ter.
43	A3	Kinellan Rd.
48	A2	Kinghorn Pl.
44	A2	Kings Bridge
43	A3	Kingsburgh Rd.
44	A1	Kings Stables Rd.
44	A2	Kings Stables Road La.
49	A3	King St.
48	B1	Kinnear Rd.
49	A4	Kirkgate
45	C4	Kirkhill Dr.
45	C4	Kirkhill Gdns.
45	C4	Kirkhill Rd.
42	B1	Kirl Loan
49	B3	Kirk St.
49	C4	Kirkwood Pl.
		London Rd.
49	C3	Kyle Pl.
		L
44	A1	Ladyfield Pl.
		Morrison St.
44	A2	Lady Lawson St.
49	C4	Lady Menzies Pl.
45	C4	Lady Rd.
44	A2	Lady Stairs Clo.
		Lawnmarket
42	A2	Lady Wynd
42	C2	Laichpark Pl.
42	C2	Laichpark Rd.
45	B3	Lambs Clo.
		East Crosscauseway
42	B1	Lampacre Rd.
45	C3	Langton Rd.
43	A4	Lansdowne Cres.
49	A3	Lapicide Pl.
49	A3	Largo Pl.
44	B2	Lauderdale St.
44	C2	Lauder Loan
44	B2	Lauder Rd.
43	B4	Laurel Ter.
		Slateford Rd.
49	B4	Laurie St.
46	B1	Lauriston Farm Rd.
44	B2	Lauriston Gdns.
44	A2	Lauriston Pk.
44	A2	Lauriston Pl.
44	A2	Lauriston St.
44	A2	Lauriston Ter.
48	A2	Laverockbank Av.
48	A2	Laverockbank Cres.
48	A2	Laverockbank Gdns.
48	A2	Laverockbank Gro.
48	A2	Laverockbank Rd.
48	A2	Laverockbank Ter.
44	A2	Lawnmarket
44	B1	Leamington Pl.
		Leamington Ter.
44	B1	Leamington Rd.
44	B1	Leamington Ter.
47	C4	Learmonth Av.
47	C4	Learmonth Ct.
47	C4	Learmonth Cres.
47	C4	Learmonth Gdns.
47	C4	Learmonth Gardens La.
48	C1	Learmonth Gardens Mews
47	C4	Learmonth Gro.
47	C4	Learmonth Pk.
48	C1	Learmonth Pl.
47	C4	Learmonth Ter.
47	C4	Learmonth Terrace La.
48	C2	Leith Street Ter.
		Leith St.
48	C2	Leith St.
49	C3	Leith Wk.
49	B3	Leith Wk.
43	A3	Lennel Av.
48	A1	Lennox Row
48	C1	Lennox Street La.
48	C1	Lennox St.
49	C3	Leopold Pl.

48 C1 Lelsie Pl.
44 B1 Leven St.
44 B2 Leven Ter.
44 A1 Lewis Ter.
    Dalry Pl.
48 C2 Liddesdale Pl.
43 C4 Lily Ter.
44 C1 Limes, The,
49 B4 Lindean Pl.
44 A2 Lindsay Pl.
    Chambers St.
49 A3 Lindsay Pl.
49 A3 Linsday St.
49 B4 Links Gdns.
49 A4 Links Gardens La.
49 A4 Links Gro.
49 A4 Links Pl.
49 A4 Linkview Ho.
48 C2 Little King St.
44 B2 Livingstone Pl.
48 A2 Lixmount Av.
44 A2 Lixmount Gdns.
49 B4 Lochend Av.
49 C4 Lochend Castle
    Barns
45 A3 Lochend Clo.
49 C4 Lochend Dr.
49 C4 Lochend Gdns.
49 C4 Lochend Pk.
49 C4 Lochend Rd. S.
49 C4 Lochend Sq.
44 B1 Lochrin Bldgs.
    Gilmore Pl.
44 B1 Lochrin La.
44 B1 Lochrin Pl.
44 B1 Lochrin Ter.
    Thornybank
46 C2 Loch Rd.
45 A3 Lochview Ct.
43 C4 Lockharton Gdns.
48 C2 Logan St.
48 B2 Logie Green Gdns.
48 B2 Logie Green Loan
    Logie Green Rd.
48 B2 Logie Green Rd.
48 A1 Lomond Rd.
49 C3 London Rd.
48 C2 London St.
42 C2 Longstone Cres.
42 C1 Longstone Gdns.
42 C1 Longstone Rd.
42 C1 Longstone Ter.
42 C1 Longstone Vw.
44 B2 Lonsdale Ter.
45 B3 Lord Russell Pl.
    Causewayside
49 B3 Lorne Pl.
49 B3 Lorne Sq.
49 B3 Lorne St.
44 A1 Lothian Rd.
44 A2 Lothian St.
44 B2 Lovers Loan
44 B1 Lower Gilmore Pl.
49 C4 Lower London Rd.
45 A3 Lower Viewcraig
    Row
    Waterston Av.
45 B3 Lutton Pl.
44 A1 Lynedoch Pl.
44 A1 Lynedoch Place La.
49 C4 Lyne St.

M

48 B2 Macdonald Rd.
45 C3 Macdowall Rd.
48 C1 Mackenzie Pl.
43 A3 Madeira Pl.
49 A3 Madeira St.
43 A4 Magdala Cres.
43 A4 Magdala Mews
47 C3 Maidencraig Ct.
47 C3 Maidencraig Cres.
47 C3 Maidencraig Gro.
44 A2 Main Point
46 B1 Main St.
48 C1 Malta Ter.
49 B3 Manderston St.
44 A1 Manor Pl.
48 C2 Mansfield Pl.

44 B2 Mansion House
    Rd.
46 B2 Marchfield Gdns.
    Hillhouse Rd.
46 B2 Marchfield Gro.
46 B1 Marchfield Pk.
46 B1 Marchfield Park
    La.
46 C2 Marchfield Ter.
46 C1 March Gro.
45 B4 Marchhall Cres.
45 B4 Marchhall Pl.
    Marchhall Cres.
45 B4 Marchhall Rd.
44 B2 Marchmont Cres.
44 B2 Marchmont Rd.
44 B2 Marchmont St.
46 C1 March Rd.
44 C1 Mardale Cres.
46 A1 Marine Dr.
49 C4 Marionville Pk.
49 C4 Marionville Rd.
47 C3 Marischal Pl.
    Queensferry Rd.
49 A4 Maritime La.
49 A4 Maritime St.
44 A2 Market St.
49 C4 Marshall Pl.
    Kirkwood Pl.
49 C3 Marshalls Ct.
44 A2 Marshall St.
    Nicholson Sq.
46 A2 Martello Ct.
49 A4 Martins Ct.
    Bernard St.
49 C3 Maryfield
49 C4 Maryfield Pl.
48 C1 Marys Pl.
    Raeburn Pl.
44 C1 Maxwell St.
46 A2 May Ct.
45 C3 Mayfield Gdns.
45 C3 Mayfield Gardens
    La.
45 C3 Mayfield Rd.
45 C3 Mayfield Ter.
48 A2 Mayville Gdns.
48 A2 Mayville Gdns. E.
    *South
    Laverockbank Av.*
48 B2 McDonald Pl.
49 B3 McDonald St.
45 C4 McLaren Rd.
44 A1 McLaren Ter.
    Dalry Rd.
43 B4 McLeod St.
44 B1 McNeill St.
49 C4 Meadowbank Av.
49 C4 Meadowbank
    Cres.
49 C4 Meadowbank Ter.
42 B1 Meadowhouse Rd.
44 B2 Meadow La.
44 B2 Meadow Pl.
    Roseneath Ter.
44 B2 Meadow Place La.
    Roseneath Ter.
43 C4 Meggetland Ter.
44 A2 Melbourne Pl.
    George IV Bridge
48 C2 Melgund Ter.
44 A1 Melville Cres.
44 B2 Melville Dr.
44 A1 Melville Pl.
    Queensferry St.
44 A1 Melville Street La.
44 A1 Melville St.
45 B3 Melville Ter.
45 C3 Mentone Gdns.
45 C3 Mentone Ter.
44 A2 Merchant St.
    Candlemaker Row
44 B1 Merchiston Av.
44 C1 Merchiston Bank
    Av.
44 C1 Merchiston Bank
    Gdns.
44 C1 Merchiston Cres.
43 B2 Merchiston Gdns.
43 C4 Merchiston Gro.

44 B1 Merchiston Mews
44 B1 Merchiston Pk.
44 B1 Merchiston Pl.
43 B4 Mertoun Pl.
44 A2 Mouse La.
45 C3 Middleby St.
44 B2 Middle Meadow
    Wk.
49 B3 Middlesfield
44 C1 Millar Cres.
44 C1 Millar Pl.
44 C1 Millar Place La.
44 B2 Millerfield Pl.
44 A1 Miller Row
44 A3 Mill La.
49 C4 Milton St.
45 B3 Minto St.
49 A4 Mitchell St.
43 C3 Moat Dr.
43 C3 Moat Ho.
43 C3 Moat Pl.
43 C3 Moat St.
43 C3 Moat Ter.
45 B3 Moncrieff Ter.
44 C2 Monkwood Ct.
48 B1 Monmouth Ter.
45 B3 Montague St.
48 B1 Montagu Ter.
    Inverleith Row
49 C3 Montgomery Street
    La.
49 C3 Montgomery St.
44 B1 Montpelier
44 B1 Montpelier Pk.
44 B1 Montpelier Ter.
49 C3 Montrose Ter.
48 C1 Moray Pl.
44 C1 Morningside Pk.
44 C1 Morningside Pl.
44 C1 Morningside Rd.
44 C1 Morningside Ter.
44 A1 Morrison St.
44 A1 Morrison Street
    Link
44 C2 Mortonhall Rd.
45 C3 Moston Ter.
44 A2 Mound Pl.
44 A2 Mound, The,
46 B2 Muirhouse Av.
46 B2 Muirhouse Bank
46 A2 Muirhouse Cres.
46 A2 Muirhouse Dr.
46 A2 Muirhouse Gdns.
46 B2 Muirhouse Grn.
46 A2 Muirhouse Gro.
46 A2 Muirhouse Loan
46 B2 Muirhouse
    Medway
46 B2 Muirhouse Pk.
46 A2 Muirhouse
    Parkway
46 B2 Muirhouse Pl. E.
46 B2 Muirhouse Pl. W.
46 B2 Muirhouse Ter.
46 A2 Muirhouse Vw.
46 B2 Muirhouse Way
43 A3 Muir Pl.
48 A2 Mulberry Pl.
    Newhaven Rd.
48 B2 Munro Pl.
    Canonmills
49 C3 Murano Pl.
44 B1 Murdoch Ter.
43 B4 Murieston Cres.
43 B4 Murieston Cres.
    La.
43 B4 Murieston La.
43 B4 Murieston Pl.
43 B4 Murieston Rd.
43 B4 Murieston Ter.
43 A3 Murrayfield Av.
43 A3 Murrayfield Dr.
43 A3 Murrayfield Gdns.
43 A3 Murrayfield Pl.
    Coltbridge Av.
43 A3 Murrayfield Rd.
42 B1 Murray Pl.
43 C4 Myreside Rd.
43 B4 Myrtle Ter.

N

43 C4 Napier Rd.
48 C2 Nelson Pl.
    Dublin Meuse
48 C2 Nelson St.
48 A1 Netherby Rd.
45 A3 Nether Craigwell
45 A3 New Arthur Pl.
44 C1 Newbattle Ter.
48 C2 New Broughton
48 A2 Newhaven Rd.
45 B3 Newington Rd.
45 B3 New Johns Pl.
49 A4 Newkirkgate
    Giles St.
48 A2 New La.
45 C3 Newlands Pk.
    Mayfield Gdns.
43 C3 New Market Rd.
44 C2 New Mart Rd.
44 A1 Newport St.
45 B3 New Orchardfield
45 A3 New Skinners Clo.
    Blackfriars St.
45 A3 New St.
43 B4 Newton St.
43 A3 Nicoll Pl.
45 A3 Nicolson Sq.
45 A3 Nicolson St.
44 A2 Niddry St.
45 A3 Niddry St. S.
    Cowgate
44 C1 Nile Gro.
49 B4 Nisbet Ct.
49 B4 Noble Pl.
44 A2 North Bank St.
44 A1 North Charlotte St.
49 C2 North Clyde Street
    La.
43 B4 Northcote St.
48 C1 North East Circus
    Pl.
48 C2 North East
    Cumberland Street
    La.
48 C2 North East Thistle
    Street La.
49 A3 North Fort St.
49 A3 North Junction St.
44 A1 North La.
46 B1 Northlawn Ter.
49 A3 North Leigh Sands
49 A3 North Leith Mill
44 B2 North Meadow
    Wk.
43 C4 North Meggetland
48 C1 North Park Ter.
48 C2 North St. Andrew
    La.
48 C2 North St. Andrew
    St.
45 B3 North St. David St.
45 B3 North St. James St.
48 C2 Northumberland
    Pl.
    Dublin Meuse
48 C2 Northumberland
    Pl. La.
    Dublin Meuse
48 C2 Northumberland
    Street N.E. La.
48 C2 Northumberland
    Street N.W. La.
48 C2 Northumberland
    Street S.E. La.
48 C2 Northumberland
    Street S.W. La.
48 C2 Northumberland
    St.
48 C2 Northumberland
    Pl.
    *Northumberland
    St.*
46 A2 Northview Ct.
47 B4 North Weber Pk.
47 B4 North Weber Pl.
47 B4 North Weber Rd.
48 C1 North West Circus
    Pl.

48 C2 North West
    Cumberland Street
    La.
48 C1 North West Thistle
    Street La.
49 C4 Norton Pk.
49 C3 Nottingham Ter.
    Nottingham Pl.

O

45 A3 Oakfield
46 C1 Oak La.
49 B4 Oakville Ter.
43 C4 Ogilvie Ter.
44 A2 Old Assembly Clo.
    High St.
48 C2 Old Broughton
45 C4 Old Dalkeith Rd.
44 A2 Old Fishmarket Clo.
    Cowgate
42 A1 Old Kirk Rd.
45 A3 Old Tolbooth Wynd
47 C4 Orchard Bank
47 C4 Orchard Brae
47 C4 Orchard Brae Av.
47 C4 Orchard Brae
    Gdns.
47 C4 Orchard Brae
    Gdns. W.
47 C4 Orchard Brae W.
    Orchard Brae
47 C4 Orchard Cres.
47 C3 Orchard Dr.
49 B3 Orchardfield La.
47 C4 Orchard Gro.
    Orchard Rd.
47 C4 Orchard Pl.
47 B3 Orchard Rd. S.
47 C4 Orchard Ter.
47 C4 Orchard Toll
43 A3 Ormidale Ter.
43 B4 Orwell Pl.
43 B4 Orwell Ter.
43 A4 Osborne Ter.
44 C2 Oswald Ct.
44 C2 Oswald Rd.
45 B3 Oxford St.
48 C1 Oxford Ter.

P

42 B1 Paddockholm, The,
44 A1 Palmerston Pl.
44 A1 Palmerston Place
    La.
    Palmerston Pl.
44 B2 Palmerston Rd.
44 A1 Panmure Pl.
48 A2 Park Pl.
48 A2 Park Rd.
45 B3 Parkside St.
45 B3 Parkside Ter.
49 B4 Parkvale Pl.
49 A3 Parliament Pl.
    Parliament St.
44 A2 Parliament Sq.
49 A3 Parliament St.
48 C1 Patriothall
    Hamilton Pl.
49 A4 Pattison St.
45 C3 Peel Ter.
45 C4 Peffermill Rd.
46 B1 Peggys Pl.
    Corbiehill Rd.
43 A4 Pembroke St.
46 A2 Pennywell Cotts.
46 A2 Pennywell Cotts.
    West Granton Rd.
46 A2 Pennywell Ct.
46 A2 Pennywell Gdns.
46 A2 Pennywell Gro.
46 A2 Pennywell
    Medway
46 A2 Pennywell Pl.
46 A2 Pennywell Rd.
46 A2 Pennywell Vill.
    West Granton Rd.
48 C1 Perth St.

48 C2 Picardy Pl.
49 B3 Pilrig Cotts.
49 B3 Pilrig Gdns.
49 B3 Pilrig Pl.
Pilrig St.
49 B3 Pilrig St.
47 A4 Pilton Av.
47 A4 Pilton Cres.
47 A4 Pilton Dr.
47 A4 Pilton Dr. N.
47 A4 Pilton Gdns.
47 A4 Pilton Loan
47 A4 Pilton Pk.
47 A4 Pilton Pl.
49 B3 Pirrie St.
49 C4 Pitlochry Pl.
Carlyle Pl.
44 C1 Pitsligo Rd.
49 A3 Pitt St.
45 A3 Pleasance
44 B1 Polwarth Cres.
43 B4 Polwarth Gdns.
43 B4 Polwarth Gro.
43 B4 Polwarth Pk.
43 B4 Polwarth Pl.
43 C4 Polwarth Ter.
44 B1 Ponton St.
49 A4 Poplar La.
47 B4 Porterfield Rd.
48 C1 Portgower Pl.
49 A3 Portland Pl.
Lindsay Rd.
49 A3 Portland St.
49 A3 Portland Ter.
North Junction St.
44 A2 Portsburgh Sq.
West Port
44 A2 Potterrow
44 A2 Potterrow Port
Lothian St.
45 C4 Prestonfield Av.
45 C4 Prestonfield Cres.
45 C4 Prestonfield Gdns.
45 C4 Prestonfield Rd.
45 C4 Prestonfield Ter.
45 B4 Priestfield Av.
45 C4 Priestfield Cres.
45 C4 Priestfield Gdns.
45 B4 Priestfield Gro.
45 B4 Priestfield Rd.
45 B4 Priestfield Rd. N.
48 A1 Primrose Bank Rd.
49 B4 Primrose St.
43 B4 Primrose Ter.
45 A3 Prince Albert Bldgs.
Waterston Av.
45 A3 Prince Regent St. 6
44 A1 Princes St.
48 C2 Prospect Bank Rd.
49 B4 Prospect Bank Gnds.
49 B4 Prospect Bank Rd.

Q
46 B1 Quality Street La.
46 B1 Quality St.
45 B3 Quarry Clo.
West Crosscauseway
49 A3 Quayside St.
49 A4 Queen Charlotte La.
Queen Charlotte St.
49 A4 Queen Charlotte St.
48 C2 Queen Street Gdns. E.
48 C2 Queen Street Gdns. W.
46 C2 Queens Av.
47 C3 Queens Av. S.
45 C3 Queens Cres.
45 A4 Queens Dr.
47 C3 Queensferry Rd.
44 A1 Queensferry Street La.
44 A1 Queensferry St.
47 C4 Queensferry Ter.
47 C3 Queens Gdns.
49 C4 Queens Park Av.
49 C3 Queens Pl.
47 C3 Queens Rd.

48 C1 Queen St.
49 A3 Quilts Wynd

R
48 C1 Raeburn Mews
48 C1 Raeburn Pl.
48 C1 Raeburn St.
45 A3 Raes Bldgs.
Holyrood Rd.
44 A2 Ramsay La.
44 A2 Ramsey Gdns.
44 A1 Randolph Cliff
44 A1 Randolph Cres.
44 A1 Randolph La.
44 A1 Randolph
45 B3 Rankeillor St.
45 C3 Rankin Rd.
45 C3 Ratcliffe Ter.
43 A3 Ravelston Ct.
43 A3 Ravelston Dykes
42 A2 Ravelston Dykes La.
46 C2 Ravelston Dykes Rd.
43 A3 Ravelston Gdns.
47 C3 Ravelston Heights
47 C3 Ravelston House Gro.
47 C3 Ravelston House Loan
47 C3 Ravelston House Pk.
47 C3 Ravelston House Rd.
43 A4 Ravelston Pk.
43 A4 Ravelston Pl.
Belford Rd.
43 A3 Ravelston Ri.
47 C4 Ravelston Ter.
48 B2 Redbraes Gro.
48 B2 Redbraes Pl.
45 A3 Reekies Ct.
49 C4 Regent Pl.
49 C3 Regent Rd.
49 C3 Regent Ter.
49 C3 Regent Terrace Mews
48 C2 Register Pl.
45 A3 Reids Clo.
45 A3 Reids Ct.
48 C1 Reid Ter.
45 C3 Relugas Gdns.
45 C3 Relugas Pl.
45 C3 Relugas Rd.
49 B4 Restalrig Pk.
49 B4 Restalrig Rd.
49 B4 Restalrig Ter.
45 A3 Richmond La.
43 A3 Richmond Pl.
44 A1 Richmond Ter.
44 A1 Riego St.
44 B2 Rillbank Cres.
44 B2 Rillbank Ter.
48 C1 Rintoul Pl.
43 B4 Ritchie Pl.
43 B3 Riversdale Cres.
43 A3 Riversdale Gro.
43 B3 Riversdale Rd.
43 C3 Robbs Loan
43 C3 Robbs Loan Gro.
43 B3 Robertson Av.
45 A3 Robertsons Clo.
Cowgate
45 A3 Robertsons Ct.
47 B4 Rocheid Pk.
48 B1 Rocheid Path
44 C1 Rochester Ter.
48 C2 Rodney St.
49 A3 Ronaldsons Wharf
Bridge St.
44 A1 Rosebank Cotts.
48 A1 Rosebank Gdns.
48 A1 Rosebank Gro.
48 A1 Rosebank Rd.
43 A4 Rosebery Cres.
43 A4 Rosebery Crescent La.
Rosebery Cres.
43 B3 Roseburn Av.
43 A4 Roseburn Cliff
43 A3 Roseburn Cres.
43 A3 Roseburn Dr.

43 A3 Roseburn Gdns.
43 A3 Roseburn Pl.
43 B3 Roseburn St.
43 A3 Roseburn Ter.
44 A1 Rosemount Bldgs.
44 B2 Roseneath Pl.
Marchmont Cres.
44 B2 Roseneath St.
44 B2 Roseneath Ter.
48 A1 Rose Pk.
44 A1 Rose Street N. La.
44 A1 Rose Street S. La.
44 A1 Rose St.
49 B4 Rosevale Pl.
49 B4 Rosevale Ter.
48 A2 Roseville Gdns.
45 C3 Ross Gdns.
49 C4 Rossie Pl.
49 B3 Rosslyn Cres.
49 B3 Rosslyn Ter.
45 C3 Ross Pl.
43 A4 Rothesay Mews
44 A1 Rothesay Pl.
44 A1 Rothesay Ter.
42 B1 Roull Pl.
45 A3 Roxburgh Pl.
45 A3 Roxburgh St.
45 A3 Roxburgh Ter.
Drummond St.
48 C1 Royal Circus
48 C2 Royal Cres.
49 C4 Royal Park Pl.
49 C4 Royal Park Ter.
49 C3 Royal Ter.
49 C3 Royal Terrace Mews
47 A3 Royston Mains Av.
47 A4 Royston Mains Cres.
47 A4 Royston Mains Gdns.
47 A4 Royston Mains Grn.
47 A4 Royston Mains Pl.
47 A4 Royston Mains Rd.
47 A3 Royston Mains St.
48 B1 Russel Pl.
48 A1 Russell Pl.
43 A4 Russell Rd.
44 A1 Rutland Ct.
44 A1 Rutland Pl.
West End
44 A1 Rutland Sq.
44 A1 Rutland St.
49 B4 Ryehill Av.
49 B4 Ryehill Gdns.
49 B4 Ryehill Gro.
49 B4 Ryehill Pl.
49 B4 Ryehill Ter.

S
44 C2 St. Albans Rd.
49 B4 St. Andrews Pl.
48 C2 St. Andrew Sq.
49 A3 St. Anthony Pl.
St. Anthony St.
49 A3 St. Anthony Pl.
Henderson St.
49 A3 St. Anthony St.
48 C1 St. Bernards Cres.
48 C1 St. Bernards Pl.
Saunders St.
48 C1 St. Bernards Row
42 B2 St. Catherines Gdns.
45 B3 St. Catherines Pl.
49 B4 St. Clair Av.
49 B4 St. Clair Pl.
49 B4 St. Clair Rd.
49 B4 St. Clair St.
44 A1 St. Colme St.
44 A1 St. Davids Pl.
Morrison St.
44 A1 St. Davids Ter.
44 A2 St. Giles St.
48 C2 St. James Pl.
42 B1 St. Johns Av.
42 B1 St. Johns Cres.
45 A3 St. Johns Gdns.
45 A3 St. Johns Hill
Holyrood Rd.
42 B1 St. Johns Ter.
45 A3 St. John St.

45 B3 St. Leonards Crag
St. Leonards La.
45 B3 St. Leonards Bank
45 B3 St. Leonards Hill
45 B3 St. Leonards La.
45 B3 St. Leonards St.
44 C1 St. Margarets Rd.
45 A3 St. Marys St.
45 B3 St. Patrick Sq.
45 B3 St. Patrick St.
44 B1 St. Peters Bldgs.
Gilmore Pl.
44 B1 St. Peters Pl.
Viewforth
48 C1 St. Stephen Pl.
48 C1 St. Stephen St.
43 C4 St. Teresa Pl.
44 C2 St. Thomnas Rd.
48 C1 St. Vincent St.
49 A4 Salamander Pl.
49 A4 Salamander St.
49 B4 Salamander St.
Claremont Pk.
45 B3 Salisbury Pl.
45 B3 Salisbury Rd.
45 A3 Salisbury Sq.
Salisbury St.
45 A3 Salisbury St.
49 C4 Salmond Pl.
46 A2 Salvesen Cres.
46 A2 Salvesen Gdns.
46 A2 Salvesen Gro.
46 A2 Salvesen Ter.
49 A3 Sandport
49 A3 Sandport St.
43 B4 Sauchie Bank
42 B2 Saughton Av.
42 B2 Saughton Cres.
42 B2 Saughton Gdns.
42 B2 Saughton Gro.
43 B3 Saughtonhall Av.
42 B2 Saughtonhall Av. W.
43 B3 Saughtonhall Circus
42 B2 Saughtonhall Cres.
42 B2 Saughtonhall Dr.
43 B3 Saughtonhall Gdns.
43 B3 Saughtonhall Gro.
43 B3 Saughtonhall Pl.
43 B3 Saughtonhall Ter.
42 B2 Saughton Loan
42 C2 Saughton Mains Av.
42 C1 Saughton Mains Dr.
42 C1 Saughton Mains Gdns.
42 C2 Saughton Mains Gro.
42 C1 Saughton Mains Loan
42 C1 Saughton Mains Pk.
42 C1 Saughton Mains Pl.
42 C1 Saughton Mains St.
42 C1 Saughton Mains Ter.
42 B2 Saughton Pk.
42 C1 Saughton Rd.
42 B1 Saughton Rd. N.
48 C1 Saunders St.
45 C3 Savile Pl.
45 C3 Savile Ter.
48 C1 Saxe Coburg Pl.
48 C1 Saxe Coburg St.
45 B3 Sciennes
45 B3 Sciennes Hill Pl.
Sciennes
45 B3 Sciennes House Pl.
Sciennes
45 B3 Sciennes Pl.
44 B2 Sciennes Rd.
45 B3 Sciennes St. E.
Causewayside
48 C2 Scotland St.
47 C3 Seaforth Dr.
49 A4 Seaport St.
44 A1 Semple St.
45 B3 Seton Pl.
45 C4 Shaftesbury Pk.
43 C4 Shandon Cres.
43 C4 Shandon Pl.
43 C4 Shandon Rd.
43 C4 Shandon St.
43 C4 Shandon Ter.

44 A1 Shandwick Pl.
45 C4 Sharpdale
Dalkeith Rd.
49 B3 Shaws Pl.
49 C3 Shaws Sq.
Gayfield Sq.
49 B3 Shaws St.
Shaws Pl.
49 B3 Shaws Ter.
49 A3 Sheriff Brae
49 A3 Sheriff Pk.
49 A4 Shore
49 A4 Shore Pl.
49 C3 Shrub Pl.
49 C3 Shrub Place La.
Shrub Pl.
45 B3 Sienna Gdns.
46 B1 Silverknowes Av.
46 B1 Silverknowes Bank
46 B1 Silverknowes Brae
46 B1 Silverknowes Ct.
46 B1 Silverknowes Cres.
46 B1 Silverknowes Dell
46 B1 Silverknowes Dr.
46 B1 Silverknowes Eastway
46 A1 Silverknowes Gdns.
46 B2 Silverknowes Grn.
46 A1 Silverknowes Gro.
46 B1 Silverknowes Hill
46 B1 Silverknowes Loan
46 B2 Silverknowes Midway
46 B2 Silverknowes Neuk
46 A1 Silverknowes Parkway
46 A1 Silverknowes Pl.
46 A1 Silverknowes Rd.
46 B1 Silverknowes Rd. E.
46 B1 Silverknowes Rd. S.
46 B2 Silverknowes Southway
46 B1 Silverknowes Ter.
46 B2 Silverknowes Vw.
45 A3 Simon Sq.
49 C4 Sleigh Dr.
49 B3 Sloan St.
49 B3 Smithfield St.
49 B3 Smiths Pl.
44 A2 Society
Chambers St.
44 A2 Solicitors Bldgs.
Cowgate
49 B4 Somerset Pl.
42 B2 South Beechwood
44 A2 South Bridge
44 A1 South Charlotte St.
45 B3 South Clerk St.
44 A2 South College St.
48 C1 South East Circus Pl
48 C2 South East Cumberland Street La.
48 C2 South East Thistle Street La.
49 A3 South Fort St.
43 C4 South Gillsland Rd.
44 A2 South Grays Clo.
45 C3 South Gray St.
47 C3 South Groathill Av.
44 A1 South La.
45 C3 South Lauder Rd.
48 A2 South Laverockbank Av.
47 C4 South Learmonth Av
47 C4 South Learmonth Gdns.
49 B3 South Lorne Pl.
44 B2 South Meadow Wk.
44 C2 South Oswald Rd.
45 B3 South Oxford St.
48 C2 South St. Andrew St
44 A2 South St. David St.
49 B3 South Sloan St.
48 A1 South Trinity Rd.
48 C2 South West Cumberland Street La.
48 C2 South West Thistle Street La.

48 A1 Spencer Pl.
45 B3 Spence St.
49 B3 Spey Street Mews
49 B3 Spey St.
49 A3 Spiers Pl.
45 B3 Spittalfield Cres.
St. Leonards St.
44 A1 Spittal St.
44 B2 Spottiswoode Rd.
44 B2 Spottiswoode St.
49 B3 Springfield Bldgs.
Springfield St.
49 B3 Springfield St.
49 C4 Spring Gdns.
44 C1 Springvalley Gdns.
44 C1 Springvalley Ter.
43 B4 Springwell Pl.
43 C4 Spylaw Rd.
44 C1 Stable La.
44 A1 Stafford St.
43 A3 Stair Pk.
43 A4 Stanhope Pl.
43 A4 Stanhope Pl.
Stanhope Pl.
49 C4 Stanley Pl.
42 A2 Stanley Rd.
49 B3 Stanwell St.
48 A3 Starbank Rd.
42 B1 Station Rd.
43 B3 Steads Pl.
44 C1 Steels Pl.
42 C2 Stenhouse Av.
42 C2 Stenhouse Av. W.
42 C2 Stenhouse Cotts.
42 C2 Stenhouse Cres.
42 C2 Stenhouse Cross
42 C1 Stenhouse Dr.
42 C2 Stenhouse Gdns.
42 C2 Stenhouse Gdns. N.
42 C2 Stenhouse Gro.
42 C2 Stenhouse Mill Cres.
42 C2 Stenhouse Mill La.
42 C2 Stenhouse Muir Dr.
42 C2 Stenhouse Pl. E.
42 C2 Stenhouse Pl. W.
42 C2 Stenhouse Rd.
42 C2 Stenhouse St. E.
42 C1 Stenhouse St. W.
42 C2 Stenhouse Ter.
44 A2 Stevenlaws Clo.
Giles St.
43 B3 Stevenson Av.
42 C2 Stevenson Dr.
43 B3 Stevenson Gro.
43 B3 Stevenson Rd.
43 B3 Stevenson Ter.
48 B2 Stewartfield
43 B3 Stewart Ter.
48 A1 Stirling Rd.
42 B1 Stoneyhill Farm Rd.
49 A3 Storries Alley
Giles St.
46 C2 Strachan Gdns.
46 C2 Strachan Rd.
44 C1 Strathearn Pl.
44 C2 Strathearn Rd.
44 C2 Strathfillan Rd.
43 A3 Succoth Av.
43 A3 Succoth Ct.
43 A3 Succoth Gdns.
43 A3 Succoth Pk.
43 A3 Succoth Pl.
45 C3 Suffolk Rd.
18 C2 Summer Bank
49 B4 Summerfield Gdns.
49 B4 Summerfield Pl.
15 B3 Summerhall
15 B3 Summerhall Sq.
18 B2 Summer Pl.
18 A2 Summerside Pl.
18 A2 Summerside St.
43 A4 Sunbury Mews
43 A4 Sunbury Pl.
43 A4 Sunbury St.
49 C4 Sunnybank Pl.
49 C4 Sunnybank Ter.
Sunnybank Pl.

49 C4 Sunnyside
45 A3 Surgeon Sq.
Infirmary St.
43 A4 Surrey Rd.
Borthwick Pl.
43 A4 Surrey Sq.
Sutherland St.
43 A4 Sutherland St.
49 A3 Swanfield
42 B1 Sycamore Gdns.
42 B1 Sycamore Ter.
44 B2 Sylvan Pl.

T
48 B2 Tanfield
48 B2 Tanfield La.
44 B2 Tantallon Pl.
44 B1 Tarvit St.
49 A3 Taylor Gdns.
Great Junction St.
49 C4 Taylor Pl.
43 B4 Tay St.
43 B4 Telfer Subway
47 B3 Telford Dr.
47 B3 Telford Gdns.
47 B3 Telford Pl.
46 C2 Telford Rd.
43 B4 Temple Park Cres.
49 B3 Tennant St.
48 C1 Teviotdale Pl.
44 A2 Teviot Pl.
44 A2 Teviot Row
49 A3 Bowling Green, The,
49 A3 Quilts, The,
44 C2 Thirlestane La.
44 B2 Thirlestane Rd.
48 C2 Thistle Ct.
Thistle St.
44 B1 Thistle Pl.
48 C2 Thistle St.
49 A3 Thomas Fraser Ct.
Cromwell Pl.
44 A2 Thomsons Ct.
Grassmarket
44 B1 Thorneybauk
49 B4 Thorntree Side
49 B4 Thorntree St.
49 B4 Thornville Ter.
49 A4 Timber Bush
49 B3 Tinto Pl.
44 C1 Tipperlinn Rd.
44 A1 Tobago Pl.
Morrison St.
49 A4 Tolbooth Wynd
44 B1 Tollcross
44 A1 Torphichen Pl.
44 A1 Torphichen St.
49 A4 Tower Pl.
49 A4 Tower Street La.
49 A4 Tower St.
49 A3 Trafalgar La.
49 A3 Trafalgar St.
42 B1 Traquair Pk. E.
42 B1 Traquair Pk. W.
48 A1 Trinity Ct.
48 A1 Trinity Cres.
48 A1 Trinity Gro.
44 A2 Tron Sq.
44 A2 Turnbulls Entry
Potterrow
42 B1 Tylers Acre Av.
42 B1 Tylers Acre Gdns.
42 B1 Tylers Acre Rd.
43 B4 Tynecastle La.
43 B4 Tynecastle La.
43 B4 Tynecastle Pl.
43 B4 Tynecastle Ter.
Gorgie Rd.

U
45 A3 Union Ct.
Richmond Pl.
49 C3 Union Pl.
49 C3 Union St.

44 A2 Upper Bow
43 A4 Upper Coltbridge Ter.
48 C1 Upper Dean Ter.
44 B1 Upper Gilmore Pl.
44 B1 Upper Gilmore Ter.
45 B3 Upper Gray St.
49 C3 Upper Greenside La.
Greenside Row
44 B1 Upper Grove Pl.
45 A3 Upper Viewcraig Row
Waterston Av.

V
44 B1 Valleyfield St.
48 C2 Vanburgh Pl.
48 C1 Veitchs Sq.
St. Bernards Row
44 A2 Vennel
45 C3 Ventnor Ter.
44 A2 Victoria St.
44 A2 Victoria Ter.
Victoria St.
45 A3 Viewcraig Gdns.
45 A3 Viewcraig St.
44 B1 Viewforth
44 B1 Viewforth Gdns.
44 B1 Viewforth Sq.
49 C4 Violet Bank
Spring Gdns.
43 B4 Violet Ter.
Slateford Rd.
46 B2 Vivian Ter.

W
49 B3 Waddell Pl.
44 A1 Walker St.
44 A1 Walker Ter.
Dalry Pl.
48 A1 Wardie Av.
47 A4 Wardieburn Dr.
47 A4 Wardieburn Pl. E.
47 A4 Wardieburn Pl. N.
47 A4 Wardieburn Pl. S.
47 A4 Wardieburn Pl. W.
47 A4 Wardieburn Rd.
47 A4 Wardieburn St. E.
47 A4 Wardieburn St. W.
47 A4 Wardieburn Ter.
48 A1 Wardie Cres.
48 A1 Wardie Dell
47 A4 Wardie Gro.
48 A1 Wardie Pk.
48 A1 Wardie Rd.
48 A1 Wardie Sq.
48 A1 Wardie Steps
Wardie Sq.
43 B4 Wardlaw Pl.
43 B4 Wardlaw St.
43 B4 Wardlaw Ter.
44 B1 Warrender Park Cres.
44 B2 Warrender Park Rd.
44 B2 Warrender Park Ter.
48 B2 Warriston Av.
48 B2 Warriston Cres.
48 B1 Warriston Dr.
48 B1 Warriston Gdns.
48 B1 Warriston Gro.
48 B2 Warriston Pl.
48 B2 Warriston Rd.
48 B1 Warriston Ter.
43 B4 Washington La.
43 B4 Washington St.
48 C2 Waterloo Pl.
43 A3 Waterside Ct.
Coltbridge Av.
49 A4 Water St.
45 C3 Watertoun Rd.
43 B4 Watson Cres.
Yeaman Pl.

44 A2 Waverley Bridge
44 A2 Waverley Market
Princes St.
49 C4 Waverley Pk.
49 C4 Waverley Park Ter.
49 C4 Waverley Pl.
44 A2 Waverley Steps
Princes St.
49 B4 Wellington Pl.
49 C3 Wellington St.
48 C1 Wemyss Pl.
48 C1 Wemyss Place Mews
Wemyss Pl.
45 A3 West Adam St.
48 B2 West Annandale St.
43 B4 West Approach Rd.
45 A3 West Arthur St.
44 A2 West Bow
49 A3 West Bowling Green St.
43 B4 West Bryson Rd.
44 B1 West Castle Rd.
43 A4 West Catherine Pl.
43 A4 West Coates
44 A2 West College St.
47 C3 West Ct.
49 A3 West Cromwell St.
Commercial St.
49 A3 West Cromwell St.
Admiralty St.
45 B3 West Crosscauseway
44 A1 West End
43 B4 West End Pl.
43 A4 Wester Coates Av.
43 A4 Wester Coates Gdns.
43 A4 Wester Coates Pl.
43 A4 Wester Coates Rd.
43 A4 Wester Coates Ter.
46 B2 Wester Drylaw Av.
47 B3 Wester Drylaw Dr.
47 B3 Wester Drylaw Dri.
47 B3 Wester Drylaw Pk.
46 B2 Wester Drylaw Pl.
47 C3 Wester Drylaw Row
42 A2 Western Corner
Saughtonhall Dr.
43 A3 Western Gdns.
43 A3 Western Pl.
43 A3 Western Ter.
47 B4 West Ferryfield
43 B3 Westfield Av.
43 B3 Westfield Ct.
43 B3 Westfield Rd.
43 B4 West Fountain Pl.
44 C2 West Grange Gdns.
46 A2 West Granton Cres.
47 A3 West Granton Dr.
47 A3 West Granton Gdns.
46 A2 West Granton Grn.
47 A3 West Granton Gro.
47 A3 West Granton Loan
46 A2 West Granton Pl.
47 A3 West Granton Rd.
47 A3 West Granton Row
47 A3 West Granton Ter.
47 A3 West Granton Vw.
44 B1 Westhall Gdns.
44 A1 West Maitland St.
45 C3 West Mayfield
44 A2 West Meadow Wk.
49 C3 West Montgomery Pl.
45 B3 West Newington Pl.
45 A3 West Nicolson St.
49 C3 West Norton Pl.
London Rd.
43 B4 West Park Pl.

47 B3 West Pilton Av.
46 A2 West Pilton Bank
47 A3 West Pilton Circus
46 A2 West Pilton Cotts.
Pennywell Rd.
46 A2 West Pilton Cres.
47 A3 West Pilton Crossway
47 A3 West Pilton Dri.
47 A3 West Pilton Gdns.
47 A3 West Pilton Gro.
47 A3 West Pilton Lea
47 A3 West Pilton Loan
47 A3 West Pilton Pk.
47 A3 West Pilton Pl.
47 A3 West Pilton Ri.
47 A3 West Pilton St.
47 A3 West Pilton Ter.
47 B3 West Pilton Vw.
44 A2 West Port
45 B3 West Preston St.
48 C2 West Register St.
44 C2 West Relugas Rd.
45 A3 West Richmond St.
45 C3 West Savile Rd.
45 C3 West Savile Ter.
47 B4 West Weberside
47 B4 West Winnelstrae
47 B4 West Woods
43 B3 Wheatfield Pl.
43 B3 Wheatfield Rd.
43 B4 Wheatfield St.
43 B3 Wheatfield Ter.
45 A3 White Horse Clo.
44 B1 Whitehouse Loan
42 B1 Whitehouse Ter.
43 B4 White Park
42 B2 Whitson Cres.
42 B2 Whitson Gro.
42 B2 Whitson Pl. E.
42 B2 Whitson Pl. W.
42 B2 Whitson Rd.
42 B2 Whitson Ter.
42 B2 Whitson Wk.
42 B2 Whitson Way
49 C4 Whyte Pl.
44 A1 William Street La. N.E.
William St.
44 A1 William Street La. N.W.
William St.
44 A1 William Street La. S.E.
William St.
44 A1 William Street La. S.W.
William St.
44 A1 William St.
48 A2 Willow Bank Row
45 B3 Windmill Pl.
49 C3 Windsor St.
49 C4 Wishaw Ter.
49 B4 Woodbine Ter.
44 C1 Woodburn Pl.
Canaan La.
44 C1 Woodburn Ter.
49 B4 Woodville Ter.
44 B1 Wrights Houses
44 C2 Wyvern Pk.

Y
49 A3 Yardheads
43 B4 Yeaman La.
43 B4 Yeaman Pl.
48 C2 York Bldgs.
Queen St.
48 C2 York La.
48 C2 York Pl.
48 C2 York Rd.
44 A1 Young Street La. N.
44 A1 Young Street La. S.
44 A1 Young St.

Z
48 A1 Zetland Pl.

EDINBURGH

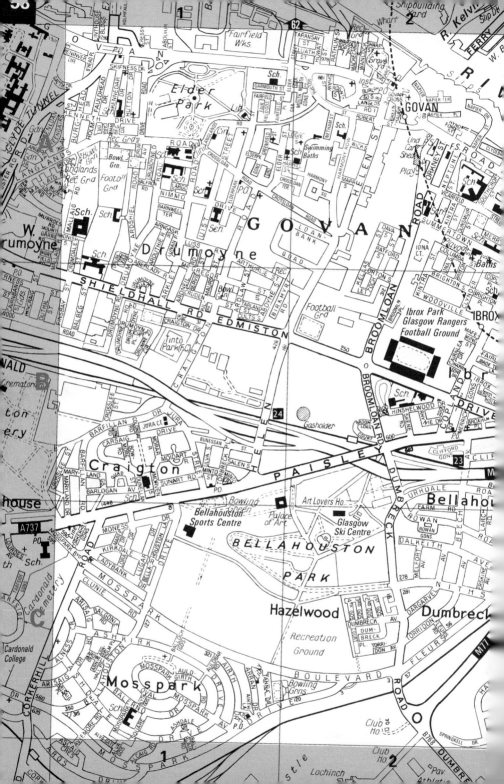

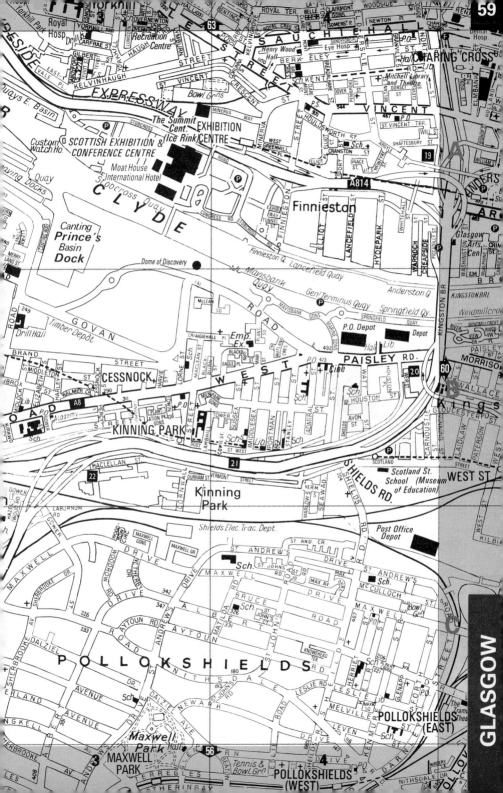

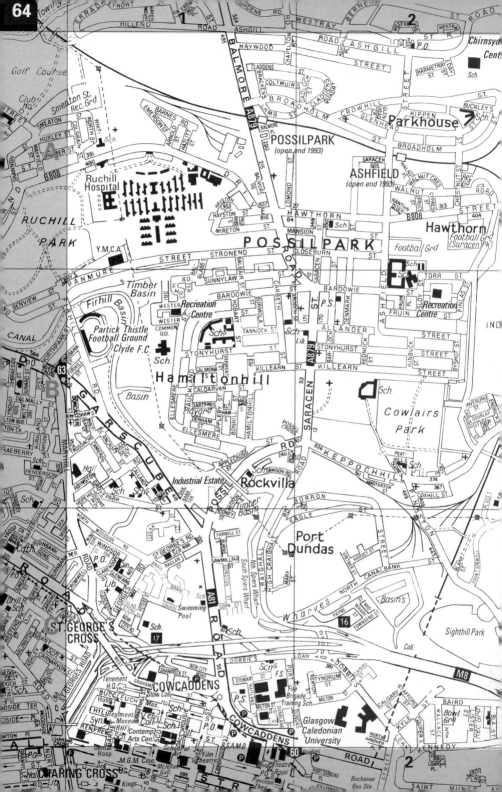

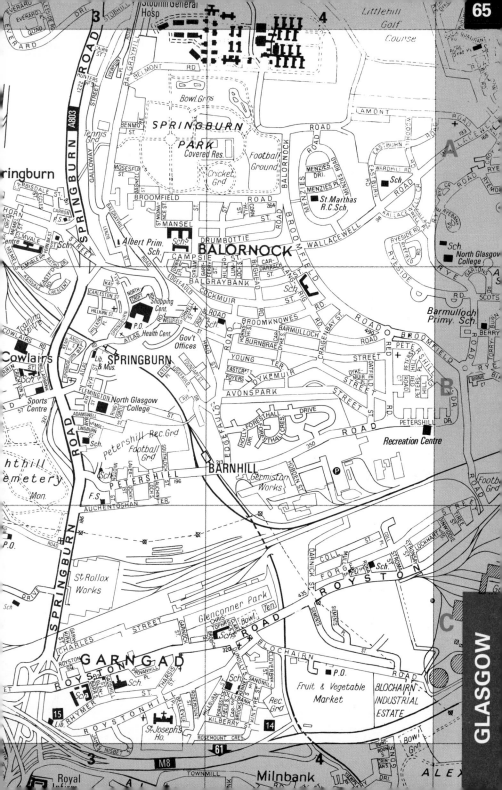

GLASGOW

INDEX TO STREET NAMES

A

62 B1 Abbey Dr.
56 A2 Abbot St.
    Frankfort St.
60 C1 Abbotsford La.
    Cumberland St.
60 C1 Abbotsford Pl.
61 B3 Abercromby Dr.
61 B3 Abercromby Sq.
61 B3 Abercromby St.
58 A1 Aberlady Rd.
64 B1 Abington St.
58 A1 Aboukir St.
58 B1 Aboyne St.
61 C3 Acorn Path
    Acorn St.
61 C3 Acorn St.
60 A1 Adams Court La.
    Argyle St.
65 B3 Adamswell St.
63 B3 Addison Rd.
60 B2 Adelphi St.
59 B4 Admiral St.
57 B3 Advie Pl.
    Prospecthill Rd.
56 B2 Afton St.
62 A1 Aigas Cotts.
    Crow Rd.
60 C1 Aikenhead Rd.
57 C3 Ailort Av.
    Lochinver Dr.
56 B2 Ailsa Dr.
62 B2 Airlie St.
56 C2 Airlour Rd.
58 C1 Airth Dr.
58 C1 Airth La.
58 C1 Airth Pl.
62 B1 Airthrey Av.
62 A1 Albany Cotts.
    Crow Rd.
61 C4 Albany St.
56 A2 Albert Av.
59 C4 Albert Cross
59 C4 Albert Ct.
    Albert Dr.
56 A1 Albert Dr.
57 A3 Albert Rd.
63 B3 Alberta Ter.
    Saltoun St.
60 A2 Albion St.
56 C1 Alder Pl.
56 C1 Alder Rd.
61 A4 Alexandra Cross
    Duke St.
61 A4 Alexandra Ct.
    Roebank St.
61 A4 Alexandra Par.
61 A4 Alexandra Park St.
64 B2 Alford St.
63 B3 Alfred Ter.
    Great Western Rd.
56 B2 Algie St.
60 C2 Alice St.
61 C4 Allan Pl.
64 B2 Allander St.
57 A3 Allison Pl.
    Prince Edward St.
57 A3 Allison St.
56 C1 Alloway Rd.
61 B4 Alma St.
58 C1 Alness Cres.
61 B3 Alston La.
    Claythorn St.
63 B3 Alton Gdns.
    Great George St.
58 C1 Alyth Gdns.
63 A4 Amisfield St.
62 A1 Ancaster Dr.
61 B1 Ancroft St.
59 B4 Anderson Quay
62 C2 Anderson St.
65 B3 Angus St.
57 B3 Annan St.
60 C1 Annandale St.
61 B3 Annbank St.
57 A3 Annette St.
61 A3 Annfield Pl.
62 A1 Anniesland Mansions
    Ancaster Dr.
61 C3 Anson St.
61 A4 Appin Rd.
64 B1 Appleby St.
64 B1 Applecross St.
62 C2 Apsley La.
62 C2 Apsley St.
63 A3 Aray St.
61 B3 Arcadia St.
    Drake St.
61 B3 Arcadia St.
61 B4 Arch St.
57 A3 Ardbeg St.

61 C4 Ardenlea St.
62 C2 Ardery St.
    Apsley St.
63 A3 Ardessie Pl.
58 B1 Ardlaw St.
56 C2 Ardle Rd.
57 B4 Ardmay Cres.
61 A4 Ardmore St.
57 B4 Ardmory Av.
57 B4 Ardnahoe Av.
57 B4 Ardnahoe Pl.
58 B1 Ardneil Rd.
58 A1 Ardnish St.
58 B2 Ardo Gdns.
58 A1 Ardoch St.
58 A1 Ardshiel Rd.
64 A1 Arduthie Rd.
58 C1 Ardwell Rd.
63 C3 Argyle St.
59 A4 Argyle St.
60 A1 Argyll Arc.
58 C1 Arisaig Dr.
58 C1 Arisaig Pl.
61 A3 Ark La.
58 B1 Arklet Rd.
63 C4 Arlington St.
61 A4 Armadale Ct.
61 A4 Armadale Path
61 A4 Armadale Pl.
61 A4 Armadale St.
61 B3 Armour St.
58 A1 Arngask Rd.
58 C1 Arnhall Pl.
58 C1 Arnholm Pl.
64 A1 Arnold St.
62 A2 Arnwood Dr.
58 C1 Arran St.
63 B3 Arriochmill Rd.
    Kelvin Dr.
61 C4 Arrol Pl.
63 C3 Arthur St.
58 A1 Arthurlie St.
57 B3 Arundel Dr.
57 A3 Ascog St.
62 A1 Ascot Av.
62 A2 Ascot Ct.
62 A2 Ashburton Rd.
58 C1 Ashdale Dr.
64 B2 Ashfield St.
64 A2 Ashgill Pl.
64 A1 Ashgill Rd.
58 C1 Ashkirk Dr.
63 C4 Ashley La.
    Woodlands Rd.
63 C4 Ashley St.
56 C2 Ashmore Rd.
63 C3 Ashton Gdns.
    Ashton Rd.
63 C3 Ashton La.
    University Av.
63 B3 Ashton Rd.
    Byres Rd.
63 C3 Ashton Rd.
    University Av.
63 C3 Ashton Ter.
    Ashton Rd.
56 B1 Ashtree Rd.
65 B3 Ashvale Cres.
65 B3 Ashvale Row E.
    Ashvale Row
65 B3 Ashvale Row W.
    Ashvale Row
63 B3 Athole Gdns.
63 B3 Athole La.
    Saltoun St.
65 B3 Atlas Pl.
65 B3 Atlas Rd.
62 C1 Auchentorlie St.
65 C3 Auchentoshan Ter.
65 B3 Auchinloch St.
64 B1 Auckland St.
58 C1 Auldbar Rd.
58 C1 Auldgirth Rd.
56 C1 Auldhouse Ter.
    Auldhouse Rd.
62 A1 Austen La.
    Woodend Dr.
62 A1 Austen La.
    Skaterig La.
62 A1 Austen Rd.
61 B4 Avenue St.
65 B4 Avenuepark St.
59 B4 Avon St.
65 B4 Avonspark St.
56 C2 Aylmer Rd.
65 B3 Ayr St.
59 C3 Aytoun Rd.

B

65 A3 Bagnell St.

61 B3 Bain Sq.
    Bain St.
61 B3 Bain St.
64 C2 Baird St.
64 B1 Bairdsbrae
    Possil Rd.
56 A2 Baker Pl.
    Baker St.
56 A2 Baker St.
60 B1 Balaclava St.
    McAlpine St.
58 B1 Balbeg St.
63 A3 Balcarres Av.
58 C1 Balerno Dr.
63 A3 Balfour St.
58 A1 Balfron Rd.
64 A1 Balgair St.
64 B1 Balglass St.
58 C1 Balgonie Rd.
65 B4 Balgraybank St.
65 A3 Balgrayhill Rd.
63 C4 Baliol La.
    Woodlands Rd.
63 C4 Baliol St.
60 B2 Ballater St.
61 A4 Ballindalloch Dr.
58 C1 Balloch Gdns.
57 B3 Ballogie Rd.
57 A3 Balmoral Cres.
    Queens St.
64 A1 Balmore Pl.
    Balmore Rd.
64 A1 Balmore Rd.
64 A1 Balmore Sq.
65 A4 Balornock Rd.
62 B1 Balshagray Av.
62 C1 Balshagray Cres.
62 B1 Balshagray Pl.
    Balshagray Dr.
61 C4 Baltic Ct.
    Baltic St.
61 C4 Baltic La.
61 C3 Baltic Pl.
61 C4 Baltic St.
56 A2 Balvicar Dr.
62 B2 Balvicar St.
63 C4 Bank St.
57 A3 Bankhall St.
61 B3 Bankier St.
57 C3 Banling Green Rd.
    Clarkston Rd.
56 A2 Bannatyne Av.
56 A2 Barbreck Rd.
    Pollokshaws Rd.
65 B3 Barcaple St.
65 A3 Barclay St.
    Balgrayhill Rd.
64 B1 Bardowie St.
58 B1 Barfillan Dr.
58 B1 Barfillan Rd.
64 B2 Barloch St.
58 B1 Barlogan Av.
58 B1 Barlogan Quad.
64 A1 Barmulloch Rd.
61 C4 Barnard Ter.
64 A1 Barnes Rd.
58 A1 Barnwell Ter.
62 A2 Baronald Dr.
62 A2 Baronald Gate
64 B1 Barr St.
61 B3 Barrack St.
63 C4 Barrington Dr.
60 C1 Barrland St.
61 B4 Barrowfield St.
57 B4 Bartholomew St.
60 A1 Bath La.
    Blythswood St.
59 A4 Bath La. W.
    North St.
60 A1 Bath St.
61 B4 Bathgate St.
57 A3 Batson St.
56 B2 Battle Pl.
57 B3 Battlefield Av.
57 B3 Battlefield Cres.
    Battlefield Gdns.
57 B3 Battlefield Gdns.
57 B3 Battlefield Rd.
62 A2 Beaconsfield Rd.
56 C1 Beafort Av.
64 B2 Beaton Rd.
63 A3 Beauly Pl.
63 C3 Beaumont Gate
60 B1 Bedford La.
60 B1 Bedford Row
    Dunmore St.
60 B1 Bedford St.
65 B3 Bedlay St.
    Petershill Rd.
65 B3 Bedlay St.
    Linsburn St.

58 C2 Beech Av.
62 B1 Beechwood Av.
    Beechwood Dr.
62 B1 Beechwood Dr.
62 B1 Beechwood Pl.
    Beechwood Dr.
62 C2 Beith St.
63 B4 Belgrave La.
    Belgrave Ter.
63 B4 Belgrave Ter.
63 B3 Belhaven Cres. La.
    Lorraine Rd.
63 B3 Belhaven Ter.
63 B3 Belhaven Ter. W.
60 B2 Bell St.
58 C1 Bellahouston Dr.
58 C1 Bellahouston La.
57 A3 Belleisle St.
65 C3 Bellevue Pl.
61 B4 Bellfield St.
61 B3 Bellgrove St.
63 A3 Bellshaugh La.
63 A3 Bellshaugh Pl.
63 A3 Bellshaugh Rd.
56 B2 Bellwood St.
63 B3 Belmont Cres.
63 B3 Belmont La.
    Great Western Rd.
65 A3 Belmont Rd.
63 B4 Belmont St.
63 C3 Benalder St.
56 B1 Bengal Pl.
    Christian St.
56 B1 Bengal St.
65 A3 Benmore St.
57 A4 Bennan Sq.
60 C2 Bentall St.
63 C4 Bentinck St.
63 B4 Benview St.
62 B1 Beresford Av.
59 A4 Berkeley St.
63 C3 Berkeley Terrace La.
    Elderslie St.
61 C4 Bernard Path
61 C4 Bernard St.
61 C4 Bernard Ter.
57 C3 Berridale Av.
56 A2 Bertram St.
58 B1 Bervie St.
56 C1 Beverley Rd.
61 B4 Biggar Pl.
61 B4 Biggar St.
60 C2 Bilbao St.
61 B3 Binnie Pl.
61 A4 Birkenshaw St.
58 B1 Birkmyre Rd.
56 B1 Birness Dr.
    Tracy St.
64 C2 Black St.
59 B3 Blackburn St.
59 B4 Blackburn St.
60 A2 Blackfriars St.
63 C3 Blackie St.
65 A3 Blackthorn St.
62 B2 Blairatholl Av.
62 B2 Blairatholl Gdns.
57 B3 Blairbeth Dr.
56 B2 Blairhall Av.
64 C2 Blane St.
63 C3 Blantyre St.
55 C4 Blochairn Rd.
61 B4 Bluevale St.
60 A1 Blythswood Sq.
60 A1 Blythswood St.
61 C4 Boden St.
65 B4 Boghead Rd.
61 C4 Bogside St.
56 A2 Boleyn Rd.
57 B4 Bolivar Ter.
57 B3 Bolton Dr.
63 B4 Bonawe St.
    Kirkland St.
61 C4 Boness St.
63 B3 Bonhill St.
61 C4 Bonnar St.
62 A1 Borden La.
    Borden Rd.
62 A1 Borden Rd.
64 B2 Borron St.
63 B3 Botanic Cres.
60 A1 Bothwell La.
    West Campbell St.
60 A1 Bothwell St.
63 C4 Bothwell Ter.
    Bank St.
63 B4 Bower St.
57 A3 Bowman St.
63 B3 Bowmont Gdns.
63 B3 Bowmont Ter.

58 B1 Bowmore Rd.
57 A3 Boyd St.
64 A1 Bracken St.
63 A3 Bracora Pl.
    Glenfinnan Dr.
63 A3 Bradfield Av.
60 C2 Braehead St.
56 B2 Braemar St.,
63 B4 Braeside St.
64 C1 Braid Sq.
64 C1 Braid St.
59 B3 Brand St.
61 B3 Brandon St.
63 A4 Brassey St.
59 A4 Breadalbane St.
59 A4 Brechin St.
57 A4 Brereton St.
56 C1 Briar Rd.
60 B2 Bridgegate
61 B3 Bridgeton Cross
58 B2 Brighton Pl.
58 B2 Brighton St.
57 B3 Brisbane St.
58 B2 Briton St.
61 B3 Broad Pl.
    Broad St.
61 B3 Broad St.
64 C2 Broadford St.
    Harvey St.
64 A1 Broadholm St.
57 C3 Broadwood Dr.
65 C4 Brodick St.
61 B3 Brook St.
56 C1 Brooklea Dr., Giff.
61 B4 Brookside St.
56 C1 Broom Rd.
65 B4 Broomfield Av.
    Broomfield Rd.
65 A3 Broomfield Rd.
    Broomfield Rd.
65 A3 Broomfield Rd.
62 B1 Broomhill Cres.
62 B1 Broomhill Dr.
62 B1 Broomhill Gdns.
62 B1 Broomhill La.
62 C1 Broomhill Path
62 B1 Broomhill Pl.
    Broomhill Dr.
62 C1 Broomhill Rd.
62 C1 Broomhill Ter.
60 B1 Broomielaw
65 B4 Broomknowes Rd.
58 B2 Broomloan Ct.
58 B2 Broomloan Pl.
58 B2 Broomloan Rd.
61 A3 Broompark Circus
61 A3 Broompark St.
60 A1 Brown St.
57 B3 Brownlie St.
59 C4 Bruce Rd.
60 A2 Brunswick St.
57 C3 Brunton St.
64 C1 Buccleuch La.
    Scott St.
64 C1 Buccleuch St.
60 B1 Buchan St.
    Norfolk St.
60 A1 Buchanan St.
61 B3 Buckingham Bldgs.
    Great Western Rd.
63 B3 Buckingham St.
63 B3 Buckingham Ter.
    Great Western Rd.
64 A2 Buckley St.
58 B1 Bunessan St.
63 C3 Bunhouse Rd.
62 C2 Burgh Hall La.
    Fortrose St.
62 C2 Burgh Hall St.
63 B3 Burgh La.
    Vinicombe St.
58 A1 Burghead Dr.
58 A2 Burleigh St.
62 A2 Burlington Av.
64 B1 Burmola St.
63 C4 Burnbank Gdns.
61 A3 Burnbank Pl.
    Drygate
63 C4 Burnbank Ter.
56 B4 Burnbrae St.
59 A3 Burndyke
58 A2 Burndyke St.
56 C2 Burnhead Pl.
63 A3 Burnhouse St.
64 C1 Burns St.
61 A3 Burrells La.
    High St.
56 C2 Burrelton Rd.
57 A3 Burton La.
    Langside Rd.

C3 Bute Gdns.
C1 Butterbiggins Rd.
A2 Butterfield Pl.,
   Pollokshaws Rd.
C3 Byres Rd.
C1 Byron La.
   Sandeman St.
C1 Byron St.
B2 Byshot St.

C
A1 Cadogan St.
C2 Caird Dr.
A3 Cairn St.
C1 Cairngorm Rd.
B1 Cairnlea Dr.
B1 Caldarvan St.
A3 Calder St.
C1 Calderwood Rd.,
C3 Caledon La.
   Highburgh Rd.
C3 Caledon St.
C2 Caledonia Av.
C2 Caledonia Rd.
C2 Caledonia St.
B3 Caledonian Cres.
   Great Western Rd.
C4 Caledonian Cres.
A3 Caledonian Mans.
   Great Western Rd.
C2 Calgary St.
B1 Callander St.
B3 Calton Entry
   Gallowgate
A3 Cambridge Dr.
   Glenfinnan Dr.
C1 Cambridge La.
   Cambridge St.
A1 Cambridge St.
C2 Camden St.
A3 Cameron St.
B4 Camlachie St.
B1 Camperdown St.
   Garscube Rd.
B2 Camphill Av.
A3 Campsie St.
C2 Canal St.
B2 Candleriggs
A1 Cara Dr.
A1 Carberry Rd.
B1 Carbeth St.
A3 Carbisdale St.
C4 Carbrook St.
B4 Cardarrach St.
A4 Carding La.
   Argyle St.
A3 Cardross Ct.
A3 Cardross St.
C1 Cardwell St.
B4 Cardyke St.
A3 Carfin St.
A3 Carfrae St.
B4 Carillon Rd.
C1 Carlaverock Rd.
B2 Carleston St.
B3 Carlisle St.
B1 Carlton Ct.
B1 Carlton Pl.
B4 Carlton Ter.
   Wilton St.
B1 Carment Dr.
B1 Carment La.
B2 Carmichael Pl.
B2 Carmichael St.
C3 Carmunnock La.
   Madison Av.
B3 Carmunnock Rd.
C4 Carna Dr.
C4 Carnarvon St.
C1 Carnbroe St.
B4 Carnoustie St.
C2 Carnwath Av.
A3 Carrbridge Dr.
   Glenfinnan Dr.
A1 Carrick St.
C4 Carrington St.
A2 Carron Cres.
A3 Carron Pl.
A3 Carron St.,
B1 Carsaig Dr.
A2 Carswell Gdns.
B2 Cartha St.
B3 Cartside Quad.
B2 Cartside St.
B2 Cartvale Rd.
A2 Castle Cres. North Ct.
   Royal Exchange Sq.
A3 Castle St.
C2 Castlebank Cres.,
   Meadowside St.

62 A1 Castlebank Ct.
   Munro Pl.
62 A1 Castlebank Gdns.
   Munro Pl.
62 C1 Castlebank St.
62 A1 Castlebank Vill.
   Munro Pl.
57 B3 Cathcart Rd.
60 A2 Cathedral Ct.
   Rottenrow East
60 A2 Cathedral La.
   Cathedral St.
61 A3 Cathedral Sq.
60 A2 Cathedral St.
61 A3 Cathedral St.
59 A4 Catherine Pl.
   Hydepark St.
56 B2 Cathkin Rd.
57 B3 Cathkinview Rd.
60 C1 Cavendish Pl.
60 C1 Cavendish St.
62 A1 Caxton St.
59 B4 Cecil Pl.
   Paisley Rd. W.
63 B3 Cecil St.
64 C1 Cedar Ct.
62 C1 Cedar La.
62 C1 Central Av.
   Broomhill Ter.
60 A1 Central Chambers
   Hope St.
60 B1 Centre St.
59 B3 Cessnock St.
58 A1 Chachan Dr.
   Skipness Dr.
61 B3 Chalmers Ct.
61 B3 Chalmers Gate
61 B3 Chalmers Pl.
   Claythorn St.
61 B3 Chalmers St.
62 A1 Chamberlain La.
62 A1 Chamberlain Rd.
62 C2 Chancellor St.
63 A4 Chapel St.
64 A1 Chapelton St.,
57 A3 Chapman St.
   Allison St.
63 C4 Charing Cross
59 A4 Charing Cross La.
   Granville St.
65 C3 Charles St.
60 B2 Charlotte La.
   London Rd.
60 B2 Charlotte La. S.
   Charlotte St.
60 B2 Charlotte St.,
59 A4 Cheapside St.
62 A2 Chelmsford Dr.
56 C2 Cherrybank Av.
62 A2 Chesterfield Av.
64 A2 Chestnut St.
56 C1 Cheviot Rd.,
60 B2 Chisholm St.
56 B1 Christian St.
65 C4 Christopher St.
57 A3 Church La.
   Victoria Rd.
63 C3 Church St.
62 B1 Churchill Dr.
61 A3 Circus Dr.
61 A3 Circus Pl.
61 A3 Circus Place La.
   Circus Pl.
58 A1 Clachan Dr.
   Skipness Dr.
64 A2 Claddens Quad.
64 A1 Claddens St.
63 C4 Clairmont Gdns.
65 C4 Clare St.
63 C4 Claremont Pl.
   Claremont Ter.
59 A4 Claremont St.
63 C4 Claremont St.
63 C4 Claremont Terrace
   La.
   Clifton St.
62 B2 Clarence Dr.
62 B2 Clarence Gdns.
64 C1 Clarendon La.,
   Clarendon St.
64 C1 Clarendon Pl.
64 C1 Clarendon St.
59 B4 Clark St.
   Tower St.
63 C3 Clayslaps Rd.
   Argyle St.
61 B3 Claythorn Av.
61 B3 Claythorn Circus
   Claythorn St.
61 B3 Claythorn Ct.
   Claythorn Pk.

61 B3 Claythorn Pk.
61 B3 Claythorn Ter.
   Claythorn Pk.
61 A3 Clayton Ter.
64 B1 Cleghorn St.
60 B2 Cleland La.
   Cleland St.
60 B2 Cleland St.
62 A2 Cleveden Cres.
62 A2 Cleveden Cres. La.
   Cleveden Dr.
62 A2 Cleveden Dr.
63 A3 Cleveden Gdns.
62 A2 Cleveden Pl.
62 A2 Cleveden Rd.
59 A4 Cleveland St.
63 C4 Cliff Rd.
58 B3 Clifford Gdns.
59 B3 Clifford La.
   Gower St.
59 B3 Clifford Pl.
   Clifford St.
58 B2 Clifford St.
63 C4 Clifton Pl.
   Clifton St.
63 C4 Clifton St.
57 B3 Clincart Rd.
64 A2 Closeburn St.
63 B4 Clouston Ct.
63 B3 Clouston La.
   Clouston St.
63 B3 Clouston St.
65 C4 Cloverbank St.
58 C1 Clunie Rd.
62 B1 Cluny Gdns.
59 B4 Clutha St.
   Paisley Rd. W.
60 B1 Clyde Pl.
60 B1 Clyde St.
58 A2 Clydebrae St.
62 C1 Clydeholm Rd.
62 C2 Clydeview
   Dumbarton Rd.
62 C1 Clydeview La.
   Broomhill Ter.
61 C3 Clydeview Ter.
   Newhall St.
58 B2 Clynder St.
61 B4 Coalhill St.
60 B1 Coburg St.
   Bedford St.
60 B1 Coburg St.
60 A2 Cochrane St.
65 B4 Cockmuir St.
56 B1 Cogan Rd.
56 B1 Cogan St.
61 C3 Colbert St.
62 A2 Colchester Dr.
64 B2 Coldstream Pl.
   Keppochhill Rd.
63 B4 Colebrook Ter.
   Colebrooke St.
63 B4 Colebrooke La.
   Colebrooke St.
63 B4 Colebrooke Pl.
   Belmont St.
63 B4 Colebrooke St.
64 A1 Colgrain St.
65 C4 Coll Pl.
65 C4 Coll St.
60 B2 College La.
   High St.
60 A2 College St.
63 A3 Collina St.
61 A3 Collins St.
58 B1 Colonsay Rd.
64 A1 Coltmuir St.
58 A2 Columba St.
61 C3 Colvend St.
61 B4 Comely Park St.
61 B4 Comley Pl.
   Gallowgate
60 B1 Commerce St.
60 B2 Commercial Ct.
60 C2 Commercial Rd.
61 C4 Connal St.
63 A3 Contin Pl.
60 B1 Cook St.
63 C3 Coopers Well La.
   Dumbarton Rd.
63 C3 Coopers Well St.
   Dumbarton Rd.
58 B2 Copland Pl.
58 B2 Copland Quad.
58 B2 Copland Rd.
60 C1 Coplaw St.
57 B3 Cordiner St.
58 C1 Corkerhill Gdns.
64 C1 Corn St.
65 A4 Cornhill St.
59 B3 Cornwall St.

56 B1 Corrour Rd.
59 A4 Corunna St.
61 B3 Coulters La.
64 C2 Couper St.
57 C3 Courthill Av.
56 B1 Coustonhill St.
   Pleasance St.
56 B1 Coustonholm Rd.
61 A4 Coventry Dr.
63 C4 Cowan La.
   Cowan St.
63 C4 Cowan St.
64 C1 Cowcaddens Rd.
59 B4 Cowie St.
65 B3 Cowlairs Rd.
64 B2 Coxhill St.
56 C2 Coylton Rd.
61 A4 Cragielea St.
57 C3 Craig Rd.
56 C1 Craiganour La.
56 C1 Craiganour Pl.
64 B2 Craigbank St.
56 C1 Craigellan Rd.
65 B4 Craigenbay St.
62 A1 Craigend Pl.
62 A1 Craigend St.
64 C1 Craighall Rd.
57 A3 Craigie St.
59 B3 Craigiehall Pl.
59 A4 Craigmaddie Ter. La.
   Derby St.
57 B3 Craigmillar Rd.
63 A4 Craigmont Dr.
63 A4 Craigmont St.
61 B3 Craignestock St.
62 C2 Craignethan Gdns.
   Lawrie St.
61 A4 Craigpark Dr.
61 A4 Craigpark
61 A4 Craigpark Ter.
   Craigpark
58 B1 Craigton Dr.
58 B1 Craigton Pl.
   Craigton Dr.
58 B1 Craigton Rd.
57 A4 Cramond St.
62 A2 Cranborne Rd.
59 A4 Cranston St.
63 B3 Cranworth La.
   Great George St.
63 B3 Cranworth St.
62 C2 Crathie Dr.
62 C2 Crathie La.
   Exeter Dr.
62 C2 Crawford St.
61 B3 Creran St.
   Tobago St.
63 B3 Cresswell La.
   Great George St.
63 B3 Cresswell St.
58 A1 Cressy St.
65 B3 Crichton St.
59 A4 Crieff Ct.
   North St.
60 A1 Crimea St.
61 A4 Crinan St.
61 B4 Croft St.
65 B3 Croftbank St.
57 C4 Crofthill Rd.
56 C2 Cromarty Av.
58 B1 Cromdale St.
63 A4 Cromer St.
57 C3 Crompton Av.
64 C1 Cromwell La.
   Cromwell St.
64 C1 Cromwell St.
60 B2 Cross, The,
57 A4 Crossbank Rd.
57 A4 Crossbank Ter.
57 A3 Crosshill Av.
58 B1 Crosslee St.
58 A1 Crossloan Pl.
58 A1 Crossloan Rd.
58 A1 Crossloan Ter.
56 A1 Crossmyloof Gdns.
62 A1 Crow La.
62 B1 Crow Rd.
64 A2 Crowhill St.
62 B2 Crown Circuit
   Crown Rd.
62 B2 Crown Circus
   Crown Rd. S.
60 A2 Crown St.
   Virginia St.
62 B2 Crown Gdns.
   Crown Rd.
62 B2 Crown Mansions
   North Gardner St.
62 B2 Crown Rd. N.
62 B2 Crown Rd. S.
60 C2 Crown St.

72 B2 Crown Ter.
   Crown Rd. S.
61 B3 Crownpoint La.
61 B4 Crownpoint Rd.
   Alma St.
58 B1 Cruden St.
61 B3 Cubie St.
   Crownpoint Rd.
61 A4 Culloden St.
58 B1 Cults St.
60 B2 Cumberland Ct.
   Gallowgate
60 C1 Cumberland La.
   Cumberland St.
60 C2 Cumberland Pl.
60 B1 Cumberland St.
60 C2 Cumberland St.
57 B3 Cumming Dr.
60 A2 Cunningham St.
   Parliamentary Rd.
63 A4 Curling Cres.
63 A4 Currie St.
57 B4 Curtis Av.
63 A4 Curzon St.
57 A3 Cuthbertson St.
64 A2 Cypress St.

D
57 A3 Daisy St.
63 C3 Dalcross La.
   Byres Rd.
63 C3 Dalcross St.
61 C3 Dale Path
61 C3 Dale St.
62 A2 Daleview Av.
64 C1 Dalhousie La.
   Scott St.
64 C1 Dalhousie La. W.
   Buccleuch St.
64 C1 Dalhousie St.
60 B1 Dalintober St.
58 C2 Dalkeith Av.
63 B4 Dalmally St.
61 C4 Dalmarnock Ct.
   Baltic St.
63 C3 Dalnair St.
61 B4 Dalserf St.
59 C3 Dalziel Dr.
59 C3 Dalziel Quadrant
   Dalziel Dr.
58 C2 Dargarvel Av.
65 B4 Darnick St.
   Hobden St.
56 A2 Darnley Gdns.
56 A2 Darnley Pl.
   Darnley St.
56 A2 Darnley Rd.
56 A2 Darnley St.
64 B1 Dartford St.
58 A2 Dava St.
61 C4 Davaar St.
62 A2 Daventry Dr.
61 B4 David St.
64 B1 Dawson Pl.
   Dawson Rd.
64 B1 Dawson Rd.
60 A2 Deanside La.
   Rotton Row
62 B2 Deanston Dr.
62 A1 Debdale Cotts.
   Whittingehame Dr.
57 C3 Delvin Rd.,
64 B1 Denham St.
64 B2 Denmark St.
59 A4 Derby St.
59 A4 Derby Terrace La.
   Derby St.
64 B1 Derwent St.
62 B2 Devon Gdns.
   Hyndland Rd.
60 C1 Devon Pl.
60 C1 Devon St.
62 B2 Devonshire Gdns.
62 B2 Devonshire Gdns. La.
   Hyndland Rd.
62 B2 Devonshire Ter.
62 B2 Devonshire Ter. La.
   Hughenden Rd.
63 B4 Dick St.
   Henderson St.
62 C1 Dilwara Av.
59 A3 Dingwall St.
   Kelvinhaugh St.
56 A2 Dinmont Pl.
   Norham St.
56 A1 Dinmont Rd.
56 B2 Dirleton Av.
57 A3 Dixon Av.
57 A4 Dixon Rd.
60 B1 Dixon St.

64 C1 Dobbies Loan
60 A2 Dobbies Loan Pl.
56 A1 Dolphin Rd.
64 B1 Doncaster St.
56 C1 Doonfoot St.
61 C4 Dora St.
62 A2 Dorchester Av.,
62 A2 Dorchester Ct.
Dorchester Av.
62 A2 Dorchester St.
61 B3 Dornoch St.
59 A4 Dorset Sq.
Dorset St.
59 A4 Dorset St.
60 A1 Douglas La.
West George St.
60 A1 Douglas St.
59 C4 Douglas Ter.
Shields Rd.
63 B4 Doune Gdns.
63 B4 Doune Quad.
56 B1 Dovecot
Shawhill Rd.
63 C3 Dowanhill Pl.
Old Dumbarton Rd.
63 C3 Dowanhill St.
63 B3 Dowanside La.
Byres Rd.
63 B3 Dowanside Rd.
62 C2 Dowanvale Ter.
White St.
58 B3 Down St.
64 B1 Dows Pl.
Possil Rd.
61 B3 Drake St.
62 C2 Drem Pl.
Merkland St.
58 A1 Drive Rd.
65 A4 Drumbottie Rd.
62 A1 Drummond Gdns.
Crow Rd.
58 B1 Drummyne Pl.
Drumoyne Circus
58 A1 Drumoyne Av.
58 A1 Drumoyne Circus
58 A1 Drumoyne Dr.
58 B1 Drumoyne Quad.
58 B1 Drumoyne Rd.
58 A1 Drumoyne Sq.
60 A1 Drury St.
63 B4 Dryburgh Gdns.
A3 Drygate
58 B1 Drymen St.
Morven St.
62 B2 Dudley Dr.
61 A3 Duke St.
58 C2 Dumbreck Av.
58 C2 Dumbreck Ct.
58 C2 Dumbreck Rd.
58 C2 Dumbreck Sq.
Dumbreck Av.
63 B4 Dunard St.
63 C3 Dunaskin St.
63 A3 Dunbeith Pl.
64 C1 Dunblane St.
61 A3 Dunchatt St.
61 A3 Dunchattan Pl.
Duke St.
60 A2 Dundas La.
60 A2 Dundas St.
62 C1 Dundasvale Ct.
Maitland St.
64 C1 Dundasvale Rd.
Maitland St.
63 B3 Dundonald Rd.
56 B2 Dundrennan Rd.
63 C4 Dunearn St.
58 A2 Dunegoin St.
Sharp St.
58 B1 Dunellan St.
58 B2 Dunlop St.
60 B1 Dunmore La.
Norfolk St.
60 B1 Dunmore St.
61 C4 Dunn St.
65 C4 Dunolly St.
61 B4 Dunrobin St.
58 A2 Dunsmuir St.
65 B3 Duntocher St.
Northcroft Rd.
61 A4 Duntroon St.
58 A2 Dunvegan St.
Sharp St.
56 A1 Durward Av.
62 C2 Dyce La.
60 B2 Dyers La.
Turnbull Sq.
65 B4 Dykemuir Pl.
65 B4 Dykemuir Quadrant
Dykemuir St.
65 B4 Dykemuir St.

E
64 C2 Eagle St.
59 B4 Eaglesham Ct.
Blackburn St.
59 B4 Eaglesham Pl.
56 B2 Earlspark Av.
60 A1 East Bath La.
Sauchiehall St.
61 B3 East Campbell St.
65 A4 Eastburn Rd.
62 B1 Eastcote Av.
65 B4 Eastcroft Ter.
61 A4 Eastercraigs
65 B3 Eastfield Rd.
59 A3 Eastvale Pl.
56 B1 Eastwood Av.
65 A3 Eccles St.
64 A2 Eday St.
62 C2 Edelweiss Ter.
Gardner St.
65 B3 Edgefauld Av.
65 A3 Edgefauld Dr.
65 A3 Edgefauld Pl.
Balgrayhill Rd.
65 B3 Edgefauld Rd.
65 B2 Edgehill La.
Marlborough Av.
62 B2 Edgehill Rd.
56 B2 Edgemont St.
61 A4 Edina St.
64 C1 Edington St.
58 B1 Edmiston Dr.
59 A3 Edward St.
Lumsden St.
59 B3 Edwin St.
60 B1 Eglinton Ct.
60 C1 Eglinton La.
Eglinton St.
60 C1 Eglinton St.
60 C1 Eglinton St.
Cumberland St.
61 B3 Elcho St.
58 A1 Elder Park Gdns.
Greenfield St.
58 A1 Elder Park Gro.
Greenfield St.
58 A1 Elder St.
58 A1 Elderpark St.
63 C4 Elderslie St.
63 C4 Eldon St.
62 C2 Eldon Ter.
Caird Dr.
61 B4 Elgin St.
63 C3 Elie St.
59 B3 Elizabeth St.
56 B1 Ellangowan Rd.
64 B1 Ellesmere St.
59 A4 Elliot La.
Elliot St.
63 C4 Elliot Pl.
59 A4 Elliot St.
56 C1 Ellisland Rd.
59 A4 Elmbank Cres.
59 A4 Elmbank La.
North St.
60 A1 Elmbank St.
59 A4 Elmbank Street La.
North St.
57 A4 Elmfoot St.
57 C3 Elmore Av.
57 C3 Elmore La.
65 B3 Elmvale Row E.
65 B3 Elmvale Row
Elmvale Row
65 B3 Elmvale Row W.
Elmvale Row
65 A3 Elmvale St.
62 B3 Elmwood Av.
62 B1 Elmwood Gdns.
Randolph Rd.
62 B1 Elmwood Ter.
Crow Rd.
59 A3 Elphinstone Pl.
57 C3 Elrig Rd.
64 B1 Eltham St.
64 A1 Emerson St.
61 B3 Emily Pl.
62 A2 Endfield Av.
64 B2 Endrick St.
62 B2 Endsleigh Gdns.
Partickhill Rd.
56 C1 Ericht Rd.
58 C2 Erskine Av.
57 A3 Eskdale St.
63 C3 Esmond St.
62 B1 Essex Dr.
62 B1 Essex La.
63 C4 Eton Gdns.
Oakfield Av.
63 C4 Eton La.
Great George St.

63 C4 Eton Pl.
Oakfield Av.
63 C4 Eton Ter.
Oakfield Av.
56 B1 Ettrick Pl.
59 A3 Ewart Pl.
Kelvinhaugh St.
60 A2 Exchange Pl.
Buchanan St.
62 C2 Exeter Dr.
62 C2 Exeter La.
Exeter Dr.

F
61 C4 Fairbairn Path
Ruby St.
61 C4 Fairbairn St.
Dalmarnock Rd.
57 C4 Fairfax Av.
58 A1 Fairfield Gdns.
58 A1 Fairfield Pl.
58 A1 Fairfield St.
58 B2 Fairley St.
62 C2 Fairlie Park Dr.
60 C1 Falfield St.
62 B2 Falkland Mansions
Clarence Dr.
62 B2 Falkland St.
58 C2 Farm Rd.
64 C1 Farnell St.
60 C2 Fauldhouse St.
63 B4 Fergus Ct.
63 B4 Fergus Dr.
65 A3 Fernbank St.
62 A2 Ferngrove Av.
62 C1 Fernleigh Rd.
58 A2 Ferry Rd.
62 C1 Ferryden St.
56 C1 Fersit St.
57 C4 Fetlar Dr.
61 B4 Fielden Pl.
61 B4 Fielden St.
62 A1 Fifth Av.
64 B2 Finlas St.
61 A4 Finlay Dr.
61 C3 Finnart Sq.
59 A4 Finnieston Pl.
59 A4 Finnieston St.
58 B1 Finsbay St.
57 B4 Fintry Dr.
64 B1 Firhill Rd.
64 B1 Firhill St.
61 A3 Firpark Pl.
Firpark St.
61 A3 Firpark St.
61 A3 Firpark Ter.
Ark La.
58 C2 First Gdns.
57 C4 Firwood Dr.
61 A3 Fisher Ct.
59 A4 Fitzroy La.
Claremont St.
59 A4 Fitzroy Pl.
Claremont St.
59 A4 Fitzroy St.
Sauchiehall St.
61 B4 Fleming St.
65 B3 Flemington St.
58 C2 Fleurs Av.
58 C2 Fleurs Rd.
60 B2 Florence St.
60 C2 Florence St.
63 C4 Florentine Pl.
Gibson St.
63 C4 Florentine Ter.
Southpark Av.
57 B3 Florida Av.
57 B3 Florida Cres.
57 B3 Florida Dr.
57 B3 Florida Sq.
57 B3 Florida St.
63 A3 Fogo Pl.
61 B3 Forbes Dr.
61 B3 Forbes St.
61 B3 Ford Rd.
61 B4 Fordneuk St.
65 C4 Fordyce St.
61 B4 Forrest St.
65 C4 Forrestfield St.
59 C4 Forth St.
61 A3 Fortingall Av.
Grandtully Dr.
61 A3 Fortingall Pl.
62 C2 Fortrose St.
56 A2 Fotheringay La.
Beaton Rd.

56 A1 Fotheringay Rd.
62 A1 Foulis La.
62 A1 Foulis St.
61 B4 Foundry Open
61 B3 Fountain St.
64 C2 Fountainwell Av.
64 C2 Fountainwell Pl.
64 C2 Fountainwell Rd.
65 C3 Fountainwell Sq.
65 C3 Fountainwell Ter.
58 C2 Fourth Gdns.
60 B2 Fox La.
60 B1 Fox St.
65 B4 Foyers Ter.
60 C1 Francis St.
56 A2 Frankfort St.
61 C3 Franklin St.
61 B4 Fraser St.
64 B2 Fraserbank St.
Keppochill Rd.
60 A2 Frederick Path
61 C3 French St.
56 C2 Friarton Rd.
64 C2 Fruin Pl.
64 B2 Fruin St.

G
64 A2 Gadloch St.
65 C3 Gadshill St.
65 C4 Gailes St.
63 A3 Gairbraid Av.
63 A3 Gairbraid Ct.
63 A3 Gairbraid Pl.
62 C2 Gairn St.
Castlebank St.
58 A1 Galbraith Av.
Burghead Dr.
65 A3 Galloway St.
60 B2 Gallowgate
62 C2 Gardner St.
61 B4 Garfield St.
58 A1 Garmouth Ct.
Elder St.
58 A1 Garmouth Gdns.
58 A1 Garmouth St.
64 C1 Garnet St.
64 C1 Garnet St.
64 C1 Garnet St.
65 C3 Garnethill St.
65 C3 Garnkirk St.
65 C3 Garnock St.
63 A3 Garrioch Cres.
63 A3 Garrioch Dr.
63 A3 Garrioch Gate
63 A3 Garrioch Quad.
63 B3 Garrioch Rd.
63 B4 Garriochmill Rd.
Raeberry St.
63 B4 Garriochmill Way
Woodside Rd.
57 B3 Garry St.
64 B1 Garscube Rd.
65 B4 Gartferry St.
60 A2 Garth St.
61 A4 Garthland Dr.
63 B4 Gartocnmill Rd.
57 A3 Garturk St.
61 C4 Garvald St.
Baltic St.
61 C4 Garvald St.
61 B4 Gateside St.
59 B4 General Terminus Quay
62 A1 George Reith Av.
60 A2 George Sq.
60 A2 George St.
65 C3 Gibb St.
Royston Rd.
63 C4 Gibson St.
63 C4 Gibson St.
59 A3 Gilbert St.
61 B4 Gills Ct.
60 C2 Gilmour Pl.
64 C1 Gladstone St.
63 B4 Glasgow St.
63 B3 Glasserton Pl.
56 C2 Glasserton Rd.
60 A2 Glassford St.
60 A2 Glebe Ct.
64 C2 Glebe St.
Kennedy St.
64 C2 Glebe St.
59 C4 Glenapp St.
62 C2 Glenavon Ter.
Crow Rd.
63 C3 Glenbarr St.
56 A1 Glencairn La.
56 A2 Glencairn Gdns.
Glencairn Dr.

57 C4 Glencroft Rd.
61 B4 Glendale Pl.
Glendale St.
61 B4 Glendale St.
62 C1 Glenfarg St.
64 C1 Glenfarg St.
63 A3 Glenfinnan Dr.
63 A3 Glenfinnan Pl.
63 A3 Glenfinnan Rd.
64 A2 Glenhead Cres.
64 A2 Glenhead St.
61 B4 Glenpark Rd.
61 B4 Glenpark St.
56 C1 Glenspean Pl.
Glenspean St.
60 B1 Gloucester St.
61 A4 Golfhill Dr.
61 A4 Golfhill La.
Whitehill St.
61 A3 Golfhill Ter.
Firpark St.
58 A2 Golspie St.
60 B2 Goosedubbs
Stockwell St.
60 B2 Gorbals Cross
60 B1 Gorbals La.
Oxford St.
60 B1 Gorbals St.
60 A1 Gordon La.
Gordon St.
60 A1 Gordon St.
63 A3 Gorstan Pl.
Wyndford Rd.
64 B2 Gourlay Path
Endrick St.
64 B2 Gourlay St.
65 B3 Gourlay St.
Millarbank St.
60 C1 Gourock St.
63 B4 Govan Cross
58 A1 Govan Rd.
57 B3 Govanhill St.
59 B3 Gower La.
Gower St.
59 C3 Gower St.
59 B3 Gower Ter.
59 A4 Grace St.
60 A2 Grafton Pl.
61 B3 Graham Sq.
63 B3 Granby La.
Great George St.
63 B3 Granby Pl.
Great George St.
63 A3 Grandtully Dr.
57 B3 Grange Rd.
56 C4 Grant St.
56 B1 Grantley Gdns.
56 B1 Grantley St.
59 A4 Granville St.
63 C3 Gray St.
60 B2 Great Dovehill
63 B3 Great George La.
Great George St.
63 B3 Great George St.
63 B4 Great Kelvin La.
Glasgow St.
63 B3 Great Western Rd.
63 B3 Great Western Ter.
63 B3 Great Western Terrace
La.
Westbourne Gdns. W
61 C3 Green Lodge Ter.
Greenhead St.
61 B3 Green St.
60 B2 Greendyke St.
58 A1 Greenfield St.
58 A2 Greenhaugh St.
61 C3 Greenhead St.
57 C3 Greenholme St.
Holmlea Rd.
62 A1 Greenlea St.
56 B1 Greenock Av.
56 B1 Greenview St.
58 A2 Greenwell Pl.
58 A2 Greenwell St.
Govan Rd.
61 C4 Gretna St.
63 B3 Grosvenor Cres.
Observatory Rd.
63 B3 Grosvenor Cres. La.
Byres Rd.
63 B3 Grosvenor La.
Byres Rd.
63 B3 Grosvenor Mansions
Observatory Rd.
63 B3 Grosvenor Ter.
64 B1 Grovepark Ct.
64 B1 Grovepark St.
57 C3 Gryffe St.

C2	Gullane St.	
	Purdon St.	
A3	Guthrie St.	

H

- A1 Haggs Rd.
- A1 Haggs Wood Av.
- A4 Haig St.
- A3 Hairmyres St.
  - *Govanhill St.*
- C2 Halbert St.
- C2 Hallside St.
- C2 Hamilton Av.
- B4 Hamilton Dr.
- B4 Hamilton Park Av.
- A4 Hamilton St.
- B1 Hamiltonhill Rd.
- B3 Hampden Dr.
  - *Cathcart Rd.*
- B3 Hampden La.
  - *Cathcart Rd.*
- B3 Hampden Ter.
  - *Cathcart Rd.*
- B4 Hangingshaw Pl.
- A2 Hanover St.
- A3 Hanson St.
- A4 Harcourt Dr.
- A1 Harhill St.
- B3 Harley St.
- A2 Harmetray St.
- A2 Harmony Pl.
- A2 Harmony Row
- A2 Harmony Sq.
- C1 Harmsworth St.
- A4 Harrington St.
  - *Maryhill Rd.*
- B2 Harrison Dr.
- C2 Harvey St.
- C2 Harvey St.
- B3 Harvie St.
- C3 Hastie St.
  - *Old Dumbarton Rd.*
- A1 Hatfield Dr.
- A4 Hathaway St.
- C3 Hatters Row
  - *Dalmarnock Rd.*
- A3 Haugh Rd.
- C3 Havelock La.
  - *Dowanhill St.*
- C3 Havelock St.
- A2 Hawthorn Quad.
- A2 Hawthorn St.
- B2 Hayburn Cres.
- C2 Hayburn Ct.
  - *Rosevale St.*
- B2 Hayburn La.
  - *Queensborough Gdns.*
- C2 Hayburn St.
- C2 Hayfield St.
- C1 Haylynn St.
- A1 Hayston Cres.
- A1 Hayston St.
- A1 Haywood St.
- C3 Hazelwood Rd.
- A2 Hazlitt St.
- B4 Heather St.
  - *Scotland St.*
- A3 Heathfield Ter.
  - *Broomfield Rd.*
- B1 Hector Rd.
- B1 Helen St.
- B4 Henderson St.
- B4 Herbert St.
- B1 Herbertson St.
  - *Eglinton St.*
- A1 Herichell St.
  - *Foulis La.*
- C3 Heron St.
- A1 Herries Rd.
- C4 Herriet St.
- A1 Herschell St.
  - *Foulis La.*
- A2 Hertford Av.
- A1 Hexham Gdns.
- A1 Hickman St.
- A3 Hickory St.
- C1 High Craighall Rd.
- B3 High St.
- C3 Highburgh Rd.
- C3 Highburgh Ter.
  - *Highburgh Rd.*
- C4 Highcroft Av.
- A2 Highfield Dr.
- A2 Highfield Pl.
- A3 Highland La.
- C1 Hill St.
- A4 Hillfoot St.
- C3 Hillhead Gdns.
  - *Hillhead St.*

- 63 C4 Hillhead Pl.
  - *Bank St.*
- 63 C3 Hillhead St.
- 65 B4 Hillhouse St.
- 65 B3 Hillkirk Pl.
- 65 B3 Hillkirk St.
- 65 B3 Hillkirk Street La.
  - *Hillkirk St.*
- 56 C1 Hillpark Dr.
- 63 C3 Hillsborough Sq.
  - *Hillhead St.*
- 63 B4 Hillsborough Ter.
  - *Bower St.*
- 62 B2 Hillside Gardens La.
  - *North Gardner St.*
- 62 B2 Hillside Gdns.
  - *Turnberry Rd.*
- 64 B1 Hinshaw St.
- 58 B2 Hinshelwood Dr.
- 58 B2 Hinshelwood Pl.
  - *Edmiston Dr.*
- 64 B1 Hobart St.
- 65 B4 Hobden St.
- 59 A3 Hoey St.
- 56 C1 Holeburn Rd.
- 60 A1 Holland St.
- 65 C4 Hollybank St.
- 57 A3 Hollybrook St.
- 60 A1 Holm St.
- 56 B1 Holmbank Av.
- 58 A1 Holmfauldhead Dr.
- 57 C3 Holmhead Cres.
- 57 C3 Holmhead Pl.
- 57 C3 Holmhead Rd.
- 57 B3 Holmlea Rd.
- 63 C4 Holyrood Cres.
- 63 C4 Holyrood Quad.
- 61 B4 Holywell St.
- 60 A1 Hope St.
- 63 A3 Hopefield Av.
- 64 B1 Hopehill Pl.
  - *Hopehill Rd*
- 64 B1 Hopehill Rd.
- 65 A3 Horne St.
  - *Hawthorn St.*
- 65 B4 Hornshill St.
- 63 B3 Horslethill Rd.
- 60 C1 Hospital St.
- 63 B4 Hotspur St.
- 59 A4 Houldsworth La.
  - *Finnieston St.*
- 59 A4 Houldsworth St.
- 59 B4 Houston Pl.
- 58 A4 Houston St.
- 60 B1 Howard St.
- 58 A2 Howat St.
- 59 B4 Howwood St.
- 61 C3 Hozier St.
- 62 C1 Hubbard Dr.
- 62 B2 Hughenden Dr.
- 62 B2 Hughenden La.
  - *Hughenden Rd.*
- 62 B2 Hughenden Rd.
- 62 B2 Hughenden Ter.
  - *Hughenden Rd.*
- 63 A4 Hugo St.
- 61 B3 Hunter St.
- 65 A3 Huntershill St.
- 65 C3 Huntingdon Sq.
  - *Huntingdon Rd.*
- 65 C3 Huntingdon Rd.
- 63 B3 Huntly Gdns.
- 63 B3 Huntly Rd.
- 60 A2 Hutcheson St.
- 60 A1 Hutchinson Ct.
  - *Hope St.*
- 58 A1 Hutton Dr.
- 63 A4 Huxley St.
- 65 A3 Hydepark Pl.
  - *Springburn Rd.*
- 59 A4 Hydepark St.
- 58 A2 Hyndford St.
- 62 C2 Hyndland Av.
- 62 B2 Hyndland Rd.
- 63 C3 Hyndland St.

I

- 59 B3 Ibrox St.
- 58 B2 Ibrox Ter.
- 58 B2 Ibrox Terrace La.
- 59 B3 Ibroxholm La.
  - *Paisley Rd. W.*
- 58 B2 Ibroxholm Oval
- 59 B3 Ibroxholm Pl.
- 62 C1 Inchholm St.
- 62 C1 Inchlee St.
- 60 A1 India St.
- 61 A4 Ingleby Dr.
- 57 A3 Inglefield St.
- 61 B4 Inglis St.

- 60 A2 Ingram St.
- 62 B1 Inverclyde Gdns.
  - *Broomhill Dr.*
- 56 B2 Invergordon Av.
- 60 B2 Inverkip St.
- 56 C2 Inverlair Av.
- 63 A3 Invershin Dr.
  - *Wyndford Rd.*
- 64 B2 Inverurie St.
- 58 A2 Iona Ct.
- 58 A2 Iona St.
- 61 C4 Irvine St.
- 56 B2 Iser La.

J

- 60 B1 Jamaica St.
- 56 B2 James Gray St.
- 60 B2 James Morrison St.
  - *St. Andrews Sq.*
- 61 A3 James Nisbet St.
- 61 C3 James St.
- 60 A1 James Watt La.
  - *James Watt St.*
- 60 A1 James Watt St.
- 57 A3 Jamieson St.
- 61 B4 Janefield St.
- 63 B4 Jardine St.
- 56 A2 Jasgray St.
- 63 B4 Jedburgh Gdns.
- 57 A4 Jessie St.
- 61 A3 John Knox La.
  - *Drygate*
- 61 A3 John Knox St.
- 60 A2 John St.
- 56 B1 Johnshaven St.
  - *Bengal St.*
- 62 A1 Jordanhill La.
  - *Austen Rd.*
- 60 B2 Joycelyn Sq.
- 63 B3 Julian Av.
- 63 B3 Julian La.
  - *Julian Av.*
- 58 B1 Jura Ct.
- 58 B1 Jura St.

K

- 60 C1 Kames St.
- 64 C1 Karol Path
  - *St. Peters St.*
- 65 B3 Kay St.
- 59 C3 Keir St.
- 63 C3 Keith Ct.
  - *Keith St.*
- 63 C3 Keith St.
- 63 B4 Kelbourne St.
- 58 B2 Kellas St.
- 60 B1 Kelty Pl.
  - *Bedford St.*
- 60 C1 Kelty St.
  - *Eglinton St.*
- 62 A1 Kelvin Ct.
- 63 B3 Kelvin Dr.
- 63 C3 Kelvin Way
- 63 A3 Kelvindale Bldgs.
  - *Kelvindale Rd.*
- 63 A3 Kelvindale Cotts.
  - *Kelvindale Rd.*
- 63 A3 Kelvindale Glen
  - *Kelvindale Rd.*
- 63 A3 Kelvindale Pl.
- 63 A3 Kelvindale Rd.
- 59 A4 Kelvingrove St.
- 59 A4 Kelvingrove Ter.
  - *Kelvingrove St.*
- 59 A3 Kelvinhaugh Pl.
  - *Kelvinhaugh St.*
- 59 A3 Kelvinhaugh St.
- 63 B4 Kelvinside Av.
  - *Queen Margaret Dr.*
- 63 B4 Kelvinside Dr.
- 63 B4 Kelvinside Gdns. E.
- 63 B4 Kelvinside Gdns.
- 63 B4 Kelvinside Ter. S.
- 63 B4 Kelvinside Ter. W.
- 65 B3 Kemp St.
- 62 A2 Kendal Dr.
- 62 A2 Kendal Ter.
- 56 B1 Kenilworth Av.
- 57 C4 Kenmure St.
- 58 A1 Kennedar Dr.
- 60 A2 Kennedy St.
- 65 C4 Kennet St.
- 62 C1 Kennoway Dr.
- 62 C1 Kennoway La.
  - *Thornwood Dr.*
- 61 A4 Kennyhill Sq.
- 63 B3 Kensington Gate
  - *Kensington Rd.*
- 63 B3 Kensington Rd.

- 59 A4 Kent Rd.
- 61 B3 Kent St.
- 64 B2 Keppoch St.
- 64 B2 Keppochhill Rd.
- 61 B3 Kerr St.
- 57 A4 Kerrycroy Av.
- 57 A4 Kerrycroy Pl.
  - *Kerrycroy Av.*
- 57 A4 Kerrycroy St.
- 61 C4 Kerrydale St.
- 63 B3 Kersland La.
  - *Kersland St.*
- 63 B3 Kersland St.
- 63 B3 Kew Gdns.
  - *Ruthven St.*
- 63 B3 Kew La.
  - *Saltoun St.*
- 63 B3 Kew Ter.
- 59 A4 Keyden St.
- 60 C2 Kidston St.
- 60 B1 Kilbarchan St.
  - *Bedford St.*
- 60 B1 Kilbarchan St.
  - *Bedford St.*
- 65 C4 Kilberry St.
- 60 C1 Kilbirnie St.
- 57 A4 Kilbride St.
- 57 B4 Kilchattan Dr.
- 57 C3 Kildary Av.
- 57 C3 Kildary Rd.
- 62 C2 Kildonan Dr.
- 58 B2 Kildonan Ter.
  - *Copland Rd.*
- 56 A2 Kildrostan St.
  - *Terregles Av.*
- 64 B1 Killearn St.
- 60 A2 Killermont St.
- 56 A1 Killiegrew Rd.
- 57 C3 Kilmailing Rd.
- 63 A3 Kilmair Pl.
  - *Wyndford Rd.*
- 56 C1 Kilmarnock Rd.
- 58 B1 Kilmaurs St.
- 57 C3 Kinalty Rd.
- 64 B2 Kinbuck St.
- 58 B2 Kinfauns Ter.
  - *Copland Rd.*
- 62 A1 King Edward Rd.
- 60 B1 King George V Bridge
- 60 B2 King St.
- 57 A3 Kingarth St.
- 57 B4 Kinghorn Dr.
- 61 A3 Kings Cross
- 61 C3 Kings Dr.
- 57 C4 Kings Park Av.
- 57 B4 Kings Park Rd.
- 57 B4 Kingsacre Rd.
- 57 B3 Kingsbarns Dr.
- 62 B2 Kingsborough Gate
  - *Prince Albert Rd.*
- 62 B2 Kingsborough Gdns.
- 62 B2 Kingsborough Ter.
  - *Hyndland Rd.*
- 57 B4 Kingsbrae Dr.
- 57 C4 Kingsbridge Cres.
- 57 C4 Kingsbridge Dr.
- 57 C4 Kingscliffe Av.
- 57 C4 Kingscourt Av.
- 57 B4 Kingsdale Av.
- 57 B4 Kingsdyke Av.
- 57 C4 Kingshill Dr.
- 57 C4 Kingshouse Av.
- 57 B4 Kingshurst Av.
- 57 A3 Kingsley Av.
- 57 C4 Kingslynn Dr.
- 57 C4 Kingslynn La.
  - *Kingslynn Dr.*
- 59 B4 Kingston Bri.
- 60 B1 Kingston St.
- 57 C4 Kingswood Dr.
- 57 C4 Kingussie Dr.
- 57 B3 Kinmount Av.
- 57 B3 Kinmount La.
  - *Kinmount Av.*
- 61 C4 Kinnear Rd.
- 59 B4 Kinning St.
- 62 B2 Kinnoul Pl.
  - *Crown Rd.*
- 56 C2 Kintore Rd.
- 58 B2 Kintra St.
- 65 C4 Kintyre St.
- 64 A2 Kippen St.
- 56 B1 Kirk La.
  - *Riverbank St.*
- 56 A1 Kirkcaldy Rd.
- 58 C1 Kirkdale Dr.
- 63 A3 Kirkhill Dr.
- 63 A3 Kirkhill Pl.
- 63 B4 Kirkland St.
- 63 B3 Kirklee Circus

- 63 A3 Kirklee Gardens La.
  - *Bellshaugh Rd.*
- 63 A3 Kirklee Gdns.
  - *Bellshaugh Rd.*
- 63 B3 Kirklee Pl.
- 63 B3 Kirklee Quad.
- 63 B3 Kirklee Quad. La.
  - *Kirklee Quad.*
- 63 B3 Kirklee Rd.
- 63 B3 Kirklee Ter.
- 63 B3 Kirklee Terrace La.
  - *Kirklee Ter.*
- 56 C1 Kirkoswald Rd.
- 63 B4 Kirkpatrick St.
- 57 C3 Kirkwell Rd.
- 59 B3 Kirkwood St.
- 57 B3 Knockhill Dr.
- 57 B3 Knockhill La.
  - *Mount Annan Dr.*
- 59 C4 Knowhead Ter.
  - *Albert Dr.*
- 64 C2 Kyle St.

L

- 63 C4 La Belle Pl.
- 59 C3 Laburnum Rd.
- 58 B4 Lacrosse Ter.
- 58 C1 Ladybank Dr.
- 61 A3 Ladywell St.
  - *Wishart St.*
- 56 C2 Laggan Rd.
- 60 B1 Laidlaw St.
- 61 C3 Laird Pl.
- 64 A1 Lamb St.
- 59 B3 Lambhill St.
- 65 A4 Lamont Rd.
- 60 B2 Lanark St.
- 63 B3 Lancaster Cres.
- 62 A2 Lancaster Cres. La.
  - *Clevedon Rd.*
- 63 B3 Lancaster Ter.
  - *Westbourne Gdns. W.*
- 63 B3 Lancaster Ter. La.
  - *Westbourne Gdns. W.*
- 59 A4 Lancefield Quay
- 59 A4 Lancefield St.
- 61 C3 Landressy St.
- 60 C1 Langbank St.
  - *Eglinton St.*
- 58 A1 Langlands Path
- 58 A2 Langlands Rd.
- 64 B4 Langrig Rd.
- 59 B3 Langshot St.
- 56 A2 Langside Av.
- 56 C2 Langside Dr.
- 57 A3 Langside La.
- 56 B2 Langside Pl.
- 57 B3 Langside Rd.
- 63 C4 Lansdowne Cres.
- 63 B4 Lansdowne Cres. La.
  - *Great Western Rd.*
- 56 C2 Lanton Rd.
- 58 C2 Larch Rd.
- 56 C2 Largie Rd.
- 58 A1 Largo Pl.
- 61 A4 Largs St.
- 57 A3 Larkfield St.
  - *Cathcart Rd.*
- 63 A3 Latheron Dr.
- 63 A3 Latheron Pl.
  - *Latheron Dr.*
- 60 C1 Lauder St.
  - *Eglinton St.*
- 62 B2 Lauderdale Gdns.
- 62 C2 Laurel Pl.
- 62 C2 Laurel St.
- 59 B3 Laurieston La.
  - *Paisley Rd.*
- 65 B3 Laverockhall St.
- 61 B4 Law St.
- 60 C2 Lawmoor Av.
- 60 B2 Lawmoor La.
  - *Ballater St.*
- 60 C2 Lawmoor Rd.
- 60 C2 Lawmoor St.
- 63 C3 Lawrence St.
- 62 C2 Lawrie St.
- 65 B3 Leckethill St.
  - *Springburn Rd.*
- 56 B1 Leckie St.
- 56 B1 Ledard Rd.
- 56 C1 Ledi Rd.
- 62 A2 Leicester Av.
- 63 A4 Leighton St.
- 60 B2 Leitchs Ct.
  - *Trongate*
- 59 B4 Lendel Pl.
  - *Paisley Rd. W.*
- 64 B1 Leny St.
- 65 A3 Lenzie St.

65 A3 Lenzie St.
64 C1 Lerwick St.
　　　Dobbies Loan
56 A2 Leslie Rd.
59 C4 Leslie St.
56 C2 Letham Ct.
56 C2 Letham Dr.
57 B3 Letherby Dr.
56 B2 Lethington Av.
58 B2 Lettoch St.
59 C4 Leven St.
63 A4 Leyden Ct.
　　　Leyden St.
63 A4 Leyden Gdns.
　　　Leyden St.
63 A4 Leyden St.
61 C4 Lily St.
63 B3 Lilybank Gardens La.
　　　Great George St.
63 C3 Lilybank Gdns.
63 B3 Lilybank Ter.
　　　Great George St.
63 B3 Lilybank Terrace La.
　　　Great George St.
57 B3 Lindores St.
　　　Somerville Dr.
62 A2 Lindsay Dr.
62 A2 Lindsay Pl.
63 B3 Linfern Rd.
58 A1 Linthouse Bldgs.
57 C3 Linwood Ct.
　　　Clarkson Rd.
63 B4 Linwood Ter.
　　　Glasgow St.
62 B2 Lismore Rd.
64 C2 Lister St.
60 B2 Little Dovehill
59 A4 Little St.
65 B3 Littlehill St.
　　　Edgefauld Rd.
64 B2 Livingstone St.
　　　Keppochhill Rd.
61 A4 Lloyd St.
58 A2 Loanbank Quad.
63 A3 Lochburn Rd.
56 C2 Locherbie Av.
56 C1 Lochlea Rd.
57 B3 Lochleven La.
　　　Battlefield Rd.
57 B3 Lochleven Rd.
56 A2 Lochside St.
　　　Minard Rd.
65 C4 Lockhart St.
57 A4 Logan St.
58 A2 Logie St.
64 A1 Lomond St.
60 B2 London Arcade
　　　London Rd.
60 B2 London La.
　　　London Rd.
60 B2 London Rd.
61 B3 Loom St.
　　　Stevenson St.
58 C1 Lora Dr.
57 B3 Lorne La.
　　　Cathcart Rd.
59 B3 Lorne St.
63 B3 Lorraine Gdns.
　　　Kensington Rd.
63 B3 Lorraine Rd.
63 B4 Lothian Gdns.
63 B3 Loudon Ter.
　　　Observatory Rd.
64 C2 Lovat St.
60 C1 Lower English Bldgs.
63 B3 Lowther Ter.
58 A2 Luath St.
57 B4 Lubas Av.
57 B4 Lubas Pl.
56 C2 Lubnaig Rd.
58 C1 Lugar Dr.
58 B1 Luing Rd.
65 B4 Lumloch St.
59 A3 Lumsden La.
　　　Lumsden St.
59 A3 Lumsden St.
58 A1 Lunan Pl.
58 A1 Luss Rd.
64 B2 Lyall Pl.
　　　Keppochhill Rd.
64 B2 Lyall St.
59 A3 Lymburn St.
63 B4 Lyndhurst Gdns.
63 C4 Lynedoch Cres.
63 C4 Lynedoch Pl.
63 C4 Lynedoch St.
63 C4 Lynedoch Ter.
63 B3 Lynn Gdns.
　　　Great George St.

M

56 B1 Macdougal St.
61 C3 Mackeith St.
58 A2 Mackenchnie St.
64 B2 Mackie St.
　　　Borron St.
60 C1 Mackinlay St.
59 B4 Maclean St.
59 B3 Maclean St.
59 B3 Maclellan St.
57 C3 Madison Av.
57 C3 Madison La.
　　　Carmunnock Rd.
61 C3 Madras Pl.
　　　Madras St.
61 C3 Madras St.
61 C3 Mafeking St.
61 C3 Main St.
59 B4 Mair St.
64 C1 Maitland St.
63 A4 Malloch St.
64 B1 Maltbarns St.
64 B1 Malvern Ct.
58 A1 Mambeg Dr.
56 C1 Mamore Pl.
56 C1 Mamore St.
62 A2 Manchester Dr.
61 B4 Manitoba Pl.
　　　Janefield St.
56 B1 Mannering Ct.
　　　Pollokshaws Rd.
56 B1 Mannering Rd.
62 B1 Manor Rd.
57 C3 Manse Brae
63 C3 Mansefield St.
63 A3 Mansel St.
64 A2 Mansion St.
56 B2 Mansionhouse Gdns.
　　　Mansionhouse Rd.
56 B2 Mansionhouse Rd.
58 C2 Maple Rd.
56 A2 March La.
　　　Nithsdale Dr.
56 A2 March St.
63 B3 Marchmont Ter.
　　　Observatory Rd.
58 C1 Maree Dr.
60 A2 Margaret St.
　　　Martha St.*
57 C3 Margarette Bldgs.
　　　Clarkston Rd.
56 A2 Mariscat Rd.
61 B3 Market St.
60 B1 Markinch St.
　　　West St.
62 B1 Marlborough Av.
59 C4 Marlow St.
59 B4 Marlow Ter.
　　　Seaward St.
63 B4 Marmion St.
61 A4 Marne St.
58 A2 Marr St.
60 A2 Mart St.
60 A2 Martha St.
61 C3 Martin St.
61 A3 Martyr St.
61 A4 Marwick St.
64 C1 Mary St.
58 B1 Maryland Dr.
58 B1 Maryland Gdns.
56 A2 Marywood Sq.
64 B2 Masterton St.
60 C2 Mathieson La.
　　　Mathieson Rd.
60 C2 Mathieson Rd.
59 C4 Matilda Rd.
60 C1 Mauchline St.
61 C4 Mauldslie St.
62 C2 Maule Dr.
58 A2 Mavisbank Rd.
　　　Govan Rd.
59 C4 Maxwell Av.
59 C3 Maxwell Ct.
59 C3 Maxwell Gdns.
59 C3 Maxwell Gro.
59 C4 Maxwell Oval
60 C1 Maxwell Pl.
59 C4 Maxwell Rd.
59 C4 Maxwell Sq.
60 B2 Maxwell St.
57 B3 May Ter.
　　　Prospecthill Rd.
57 A3 Maybank La.
　　　Victoria Rd.
57 A3 Maybank St.
63 A4 Mayfield St.
60 B1 McAlpine St.
56 B1 McArthur St.
　　　Pleasance St.
60 A2 McAslin Ct.
61 A3 McAslin St.

59 C4 McCulloch St.
61 B3 McFarlane St.
58 B1 McGregor St.
61 A3 McIntosh Ct.
　　　McIntosh St.
61 A3 McIntosh St.
59 A4 McIntyre St.
59 B3 McLean Sq.
57 B3 McLennan St.
60 C2 McNeil St.
61 C3 McPhail St.
64 C1 McPhater St.
　　　Dunblane St.
60 B2 McPherson St.
　　　High St.
62 C2 Meadow Rd.
61 A4 Meadowpark St.
62 C2 Meadowside St.
61 C3 Megan Gate
　　　Megan St.
61 C3 Megan St.
61 B3 Melbourne St.
58 A1 Meldon Pl.
56 C2 Melfort Av.
63 B4 Melrose Gdns.
64 C1 Melrose St.
　　　Queens Cres.
63 A3 Melvaig Pl.
60 A2 Melville Ct.
　　　Brunswick St.
59 C4 Melville St.
65 A3 Memel St.
57 C3 Menock Rd.
65 A4 Menzies Dr.
65 A4 Menzies Pl.
65 A4 Menzies St.
60 B2 Merchant La.
　　　Clyde St.
62 C2 Merkland Ct.
　　　Vine St.
62 C2 Merkland St.
58 B2 Merrick Gdns.
56 C1 Merryburn Av., Giff.
59 A3 Merryland Pl.
58 A2 Merryland St.
56 C1 Merrylea Cres.,
　　　Giff.
56 C1 Merrylee Rd.
56 C1 Merryvale Pl., Giff.
60 B1 Metropole La.
　　　Howard St.
57 C4 Midcroft Av.
59 B4 Middlesex St.
59 B3 Middleton St.
59 B1 Midland St.
59 B3 Midlock St.
56 A1 Midlothian Dr.
65 B3 Midton St.
64 C2 Midwharf St.
63 A3 Migvie Pl.
　　　Wyndford Rd.
60 C1 Milan St.
61 C3 Mill Cres.
61 B3 Mill Road Gdns.
61 C3 Mill St.
65 B3 Millarbank St.
56 B2 Millbrae Cres.
56 B2 Millbrae Rd.
　　　Millbrae Rd.
56 B2 Millbrae Rd.
65 C4 Millburn St.
60 A2 Miller St.
61 C4 Millerfield Pl.
61 C4 Millerfield Rd.
61 B4 Millerston St.
61 B3 Millpond Dr.
57 B3 Millport Av.
61 B3 Millroad Dr.
61 B3 Millroad St.
61 A4 Milnbank St.
62 A1 Milner Rd.
59 B4 Milnpark St.
64 C2 Milton St.
56 A2 Minard Rd.
59 A4 Minerva St.
59 A4 Minerva Way
63 B3 Mingarry La.
　　　Clouston St.
63 B3 Mingarry St.
58 B1 Minto Cres.
58 B1 Minto St.
64 A1 Mireton St.
63 B3 Mirrlees Dr.
63 B3 Mirrlees La.
　　　Redlands Rd.
60 A1 Mitchell La.
　　　Buchanan St.
60 A1 Mitchell St.
62 B1 Mitre La.

62 B1 Mitre La. W.
　　　Mitre La.
62 B1 Mitre Rd.
56 C2 Mochrum Rd.
60 C2 Moffat St.
58 B1 Moidart Cres.
　　　Moidart Rd.
58 B1 Moidart Pl.
　　　Moidart Rd.
58 B1 Moidart Rd.
60 B2 Moir La.
　　　Moir St.
60 B2 Moir St.
60 B2 Molendinar St.
65 B3 Mollinsburn St.
64 C1 Moncrieff Pl.
　　　North Woodside Rd.
64 C1 Moncrieff St.
　　　Balnain St.
61 B3 Moncur St.
58 C1 Moness Dr.
62 B2 Monkscroft Av.
62 B2 Monkscroft Gdns.
　　　Monkscroft Av.
62 B2 Monkscroft St.
　　　Kirkmichael Av.
62 A2 Monmouth Av.
57 C3 Monreith Rd. E.
56 C1 Monreith Rd.
62 B2 Montague La.
63 C4 Montague St.
62 B2 Montague Ter.
　　　Hyndland Rd.
61 B3 Monteith Pl.
61 B3 Monteith Row
61 B3 Monteith Row La.
　　　Monteith Row
57 B4 Montford Av.
57 B3 Montgomery La.
　　　Somerville Dr.
61 C3 Montgomery St.
　　　London Rd.
60 A2 Montrose St.
60 A1 Moodies Ct.
　　　Argyle St.
61 B4 Moore St.
　　　Gallowgate
58 B1 Morar Rd.
56 A2 Moray Pl.
61 C4 Mordaunt St.
60 C1 Morgan Ms.
63 B3 Morley St.
62 C1 Morna Pl.
　　　Victoria Park Dr. S.
65 B3 Morrin Path
　　　Crichton St.
61 A3 Morrin Sq.
　　　Collins St.
65 B3 Morrin St.
61 B3 Morris Pl.
60 B1 Morrison St.
60 A1 Morrisons Ct.
　　　Argyle St.
63 B4 Mortimer St.
　　　Hotspur St.
56 A1 Morton Gdns.
58 B1 Morven St.
65 A3 Mosesfield St.
65 A3 Mosesfield Ter.
　　　Balgray Hill Rd.
56 A2 Moss-side Rd.
56 C1 Mossgiel Rd.
58 C1 Mosspark Av.
58 C1 Mosspark Boulevard
58 C1 Mosspark Oval
58 C1 Mosspark Sq.
57 B3 Mount Annan Dr.
63 B4 Mount St.
56 B2 Mount Stuart St.
61 B4 Mountainblue St.
63 C3 Moy St.
　　　Church St.
65 B3 Muir St.
62 C2 Muirhead St.
　　　Purdon St.
56 A2 Muirhouse St.
　　　Pollokshaws Rd.
62 C2 Muirpark St.
56 C2 Muirskeith Cres.
56 C2 Muirskeith Pl.
56 C2 Muirskeith Rd.
56 C1 Mulberry Rd.
65 C4 Mull St.
62 A1 Munro La.
62 A1 Munro Pl.
62 A1 Munro Rd.
63 B4 Murano St.
65 A3 Murdoch St.
　　　Lenzie St.
61 C3 Muslin St.
57 B4 Myrtle Hill La.

57 B4 Myrtle Hill Vw.
57 A4 Myrtle Pk.
57 B4 Myrtle Pl.

N

60 C2 Naburn St.
63 C3 Nairn St.
64 B1 Nansen St.
58 A2 Napier Dr.
58 A2 Napier Pl.
58 A2 Napier Rd.
59 A3 Napier St.
58 A2 Napier Ter.
63 C4 Napiershall La.
　　　Napiershall St.
63 C4 Napiershall Pl.
　　　Napiershall St.
63 C4 Napiershall St.
62 B1 Naseby Av.
60 A2 Nelson Mandela Pl.
60 B1 Nelson St.
63 B4 Nelson Ter.
　　　Glasgow St.
58 A2 Neptune St.
58 A2 Netham St.
59 C3 Netherby Rd.
64 C1 New City Rd.
60 B2 New Wynd
59 C3 Newark Dr.
56 B1 Newburgh St.
57 C4 Newcroft Dr.
61 C3 Newhall St.
56 C2 Newlands Rd.
56 C2 Newlandsfield Rd.
63 C4 Newton Pl.
59 A4 Newton Ter.
　　　Sauchiehall St.
63 C4 Newton Terrace La.
　　　Elderslie St.
60 A2 Nicholas St.
60 B1 Nicholson La.
　　　Nicholson St.
60 B1 Nicholson St.
60 B1 Nicholson St.
56 A2 Niddrie Rd.
56 A2 Niddrie Sq.
56 A1 Nigel Gdns.
58 A1 Nimmo Dr.
56 A2 Nithsdale Dr.
59 C4 Nithsdale Pl.
　　　Sheilds Rd.
58 C2 Nithsdale Rd.
56 A2 Nithsdale St.
63 A3 Niven St.
62 B1 Norby Rd.
57 B3 Norfield Dr.
60 B1 Norfolk Ct.
60 B1 Norfolk La.
　　　Norfolk St.
60 B1 Norfolk St.
56 A2 Norham St.
61 C3 Norman St.
64 C2 North Canalbank St.
63 C4 North Claremont St.
60 A2 North Court La.
　　　Buchanan St.
60 B2 North Dr.
62 B2 North Gardner St.
64 C2 North Hanover Pl.
60 A2 North Hanover St.
63 B4 North Park St.
59 A4 North Pl.
　　　North St.
60 A2 North Portland St.
60 A2 North Queen St.
　　　George Sq.
59 A4 North St.
64 C2 North Wallace St.
63 B4 North Woodside Rd.
62 A2 Northampton Dr.
62 A2 Northampton La.
　　　Northampton Dr.
65 B3 Northcroft Rd.
63 B4 Northpark Ter.
　　　Hamilton Dr.
63 B4 Northumberland St.
62 C2 Norval St.
62 A2 Norwich Dr.
63 C4 Norwood Ter.
　　　Southpark Av.
62 A2 Nottingham Av.
62 A2 Nottingham La.
　　　Northampton Dr.
62 B2 Novar Dr.
61 C4 Nuneaton St.
56 A2 Nursery La.
56 A2 Nursery St.
　　　Pollokshaws Rd.
56 A2 Nursery Street La.
　　　Nithsdale St.

O
B1 Oakbank La.
B1 Oakbank Ter.
C4 Oakfield Av.
C4 Oakfield Ter.
  Oakfield Av.
A3 Oakley Ter.
B4 Oatfield St.
B4 Oban Ct.
B4 Oban Dr.
B3 Observatory La.
  Observatory Rd.
B3 Observatory St.
C3 Old Castle Rd.
C3 Old Dalmarnock Rd.
C3 Old Dumbarton Rd.
C2 Old Rutherglen Rd.
B2 Old Wynd
C4 Olrig Ter.
  Shields Rd.
B3 Olympia St.
A4 Onslow Dr.
A4 Onslow Sq.
  Onslow Dr.
B4 Oran Gate
A4 Oran Gdns.
A4 Oran Pl.
A4 Oran St.
C3 Orchy St.
C2 Oregon Pl.
A2 Orkney Pl.
  Orkney St.
A2 Orkney St.
B1 Orleans Av.
B1 Orleans La.
B3 Orr Pl.
B3 Orr St.
B3 Orton St.
B3 Orwell St.
B2 Osborn Ter.
  Copland Rd.
B2 Osborne St.
C3 Osborne Vill.
  Holmhead Rd.
C2 Ossian Rd.
B1 Oswald La.
  Oswald St.
B1 Oswald St.
C4 Otago La.
  Otago St.
C4 Otago La. N.
  Otago St.
C4 Otago St.
C2 Otter La.
  Castlebank St.
B2 Overdale Av.
B2 Overdale Gdns.
B2 Overdale St.
B2 Overdale Vills.
  Overdale St.
A3 Overnewton Pl.
  Kelvinhaugh St.
A3 Overnewton Sq.
C3 Overnewton St.
B4 Overtown St.
C4 Overwood Dr.
B1 Oxford La.
B1 Oxford St.

P
B4 Paisley Rd.
B3 Palermo St.
A3 Palmerston Pl.
  Kelvinhaugh St.
B1 Panmure St.
C4 Park Av.
C4 Park Circus C3
C4 Park Circus La.
  Lynedoch Pl.
C4 Park Circus Pl.
C4 Park Dr.
C4 Park Gardens La.
  Clifton St.
C4 Park Gate
C4 Park Gdns.
B3 Park La.
C4 Park Quad.
C4 Park Rd.
C4 Park St. S.
C4 Park Ter.
A2 Park Ter.
  Queens Dr.
C1 Parker St.
C4 Parkgrove Ter.
A4 Parkgrove Ter. La.
  Derby St.
B1 Parkhill Rd.
B4 Parkholm La.
  Paisley Rd.
A3 Parkhouse La.

61 A3 Parliament Rd.
60 A2 Parliamentary Rd.
60 B2 Parnie St.
61 A3 Parson St.
63 C3 Partick Bridge St.
62 B2 Partickhill Av.
62 B2 Partickhill Ct.
  Partickhill Av.
62 B2 Partickhill Rd.
60 B1 Paterson St.
61 C4 Patna St.
61 A4 Paton St.
64 C2 Payne St.
58 A2 Pearce La.
64 B2 Peathill St.
62 C2 Peel La.
  Burgh Hall St.
62 C2 Peel St.
59 A4 Pembroke St.
58 A1 Peninver Dr.
62 A2 Penrith St.
61 C3 Pentland Pl.
56 C1 Pentland Rd.
59 B3 Percy St.
65 B4 Petershill Ct.
65 B4 Petershill Dr.
65 B4 Petershill Pl.
65 B3 Petershill Rd.
56 A1 Peveril Av.
64 C1 Phoenix Park Ter.
  Corn St.
64 C1 Phoenix Rd.
  Great Western Rd.
59 A4 Piccadilly St.
60 C2 Pine Pl.
64 C2 Pinkston Dr.
64 B2 Pinkston Rd.
61 C3 Pirn St.
60 A1 Pitt St.
59 B4 Plantation Pl.
  Govan Rd.
59 B4 Plantation Sq.
61 C4 Playfair St.
56 B1 Pleasance La.
56 B1 Pleasance St.
57 A4 Polmadie Av.
57 A4 Polmadie St.
57 A4 Polmadie St.
62 B2 Polwarth Gdns.
  Novar Dr.
62 B2 Polwarth La.
  Novar Dr.
62 B2 Polwarth St.
62 B1 Poplar Av.
58 B2 Poplar Rd.
  Urrdale Rd.
61 C3 Poplin St.
64 C2 Port Dundas Rd.
59 A4 Port St.
63 C4 Portman Pl.
  Cowan St.
59 B4 Portman St.
60 B1 Portugal La.
  Bedford St.
60 B1 Portugal St.
  Norfolk Ct.
64 B1 Possil Cross
64 B1 Possil Rd.
57 A3 Preston St.
62 B2 Prince Albert Rd.
57 A3 Prince Edward St.
63 B3 Prince of Wales Ter.
  Byres Rd.
62 B2 Princes Gdns.
63 B3 Princes Pl.
63 B3 Princes Ter.
56 B1 Prospect Rd.
57 A4 Prospecthill Circus
57 B4 Prospecthill Dr.
57 B3 Prospecthill Rd.
57 B4 Prospecthill Sq.
65 C3 Provanhill Pl.
62 C2 Purdon St.

Q
56 C2 Quadrant Rd.
60 A1 Queen Arc.
  Renfrew St.
63 B4 Queen Margaret Cres.
  Hamilton Dr.
63 B4 Queen Margaret Ct.
63 B3 Queen Margaret Dr.
63 B4 Queen Margaret Dr.
57 A3 Queen Mary Av.
61 C3 Queen Mary St.
56 A2 Queen Sq.
60 A2 Queen St.
64 C1 Queens Cres.
63 B4 Queens Cross
56 A2 Queens Dr.

57 A3 Queens Drive La.
63 B3 Queens Gdns.
  Victoria Crescent
  Rd.
57 A3 Queens Park Av.
63 B3 Queens Pl.
62 B2 Queensborough
  Gdns.
65 B3 Queenshill St.
56 A2 Quentin St.

R
59 A4 Radnor St.
  Argyle St.
63 B4 Raeberry St.
64 C1 Raglan St.
62 B1 Randolph Rd.
57 C3 Rannoch St.
58 A2 Ratford St.
58 A2 Rathlin St.
65 A3 Ratho Dr.
56 B1 Ravenshall Rd.
56 A1 Ravenswood Dr.
65 B4 Red Rd.
65 B4 Red Road Ct.
61 B3 Redan St.
63 B3 Redlands La.
  Kirkle Rd.
63 B3 Redlands Rd.
63 B3 Redlands Ter.
63 B3 Redlands Terrace La.
  Julian Av.
64 A1 Redmoss St.
64 B2 Rednock St.
63 C3 Regent Moray St.
56 A2 Regent Park Sq.
56 A2 Regent Park Ter.
  Pollokshaws Rd.
56 B1 Regwood St.
61 C3 Reid Pl.
  Muslin St.
61 C3 Reid St.
65 B3 Reidhouse St.
  Muir St.
61 B3 Reidvale St.
60 A1 Renfield St.
60 A1 Renfrew Ct.
  Renfrew St.
60 A1 Renfrew La.
  Renfield St.
64 C1 Renfrew St.
64 C2 Renton St.
59 B4 Renwick St.
  Scotland St.
57 C3 Rhannan Rd.
57 C3 Rhannan Ter.
65 C3 Rhymer St.
58 B2 Rhynie Dr.
57 A4 Riccarton St.
60 A2 Richmond St.
61 B4 Rimsdale St.
65 B3 Ringford St.
62 A2 Ripon Dr.
61 B3 Risk St.
60 C1 Ritchie St.
56 B2 River Rd.
56 B1 Riverbank St.
56 B1 Riverford Rd.
56 B2 Riverside Rd.
60 B1 Riverview Av.
  West St.
60 B1 Riverview St.
60 B1 Riverview Pl.
  Riverview Dr.
65 B3 Robb St.
58 A2 Robert St.
56 A1 Roberton Av.
60 A1 Robertson La.
  Robertson St.
60 A1 Robertson St.
57 A3 Robson Gro.
64 B1 Rock St.
61 B4 Rockbank Pl.
  Broad St.
61 B4 Rockbank St.
61 C3 Rockcliffe St.
64 C1 Rodney St.
61 A4 Roebank St.
61 B3 Rogart St.
63 B3 Rokeby Ter.
  Great Western Rd.
57 C4 Romney Av.
62 A1 Rose Cotts.
  Crow Rd.
60 A1 Rose St.
65 C4 Rosemount Cres.
65 C3 Rosemount St.
59 B4 Rosemount Ter.
  Paisley Rd. W.
62 C2 Rosevale St.

61 A4 Roslea Dr.
58 A2 Rosneath St.
60 B2 Ross St.
56 B1 Rossendale Rd.
63 B3 Rosslyn Ter.
  Horslethill Rd.
56 C1 Rostan Rd.
62 A2 Rottenrow East
62 B2 Rowallan Gdns.
62 B2 Rowallan La. E.
  Churchill Dr.
62 B2 Rowallan La.
  Churchill Dr.
58 C2 Rowan Gdns.
58 C2 Rowan Rd.
61 B4 Rowchester St.
63 B3 Roxburgh La.
  Saltoun St.
63 B3 Roxburgh St.
64 B2 Roy St.
60 A2 Royal Bank Pl.
  Buchanan St.
63 C4 Royal Cres.
57 A3 Royal Cres.
60 A2 Royal Exchange
  Bldgs.
  Royal Exchange Sq.
60 A2 Royal Exchange Ct.
  Queen St.
60 A2 Royal Exchange Sq.
63 C4 Royal Ter.
57 A3 Royal Ter.
  Queens Dr.
63 C4 Royal Terrace La.
  North Claremont St.
65 C3 Royston Hill.
65 C3 Royston Rd.
65 C3 Royston Sq.
61 C4 Ruby St.
63 A4 Ruchill Pl.
63 A4 Ruchill St.
57 B3 Ruel St.
61 C3 Rumford St.
63 C4 Rupert St.
65 B4 Rushyhill St.
  Cockmuir St.
63 B4 Ruskin La.
63 B3 Ruskin Pl.
  Great Western Rd.
63 B4 Ruskin Ter.
62 C2 Russell St.
  Vine St.
60 A1 Rutherford La.
  Hope St.
60 B2 Rutherglen Rd.
63 B3 Ruthven La.
  Dowanside Rd.
63 B3 Ruthven St.
59 B4 Rutland Cres.
59 B4 Rutland La.
  Govan Rd.
59 B4 Rutland Pl.
65 A4 Ryefield Rd.
65 A4 Ryeside Rd.

S
62 A1 Sackville Av.
62 A1 Sackville La.
  Sackville Av.
59 C4 St. Andrews Cres.
60 C1 St. Andrews Cross
56 A1 St. Andrews Drive
60 B2 St. Andrews La.
  Gallowgate
59 C4 St. Andrews Rd.
60 B2 St. Andrews Sq.
60 B2 St. Andrews St.
56 B1 St. Brides Rd.
63 C4 St. Clair St.
  Woodside Rd.
60 B1 St. Enoch Sq.
60 A1 St. Enoch Wynd
  Argyle St.
64 C1 St. Georges Cross
64 C1 St. Georges Pl.
  St. Georges Rd.
64 C1 St. Georges Rd.
60 A2 St. James Rd.
59 C4 St. Johns Ct.
59 C4 St. Johns Quad.
59 C4 St. Johns Rd.
63 C4 St. Johns Ter.
  Southpark Av.
61 B3 St. Jospehs Pl.
  Abercromby St.
58 A1 St. Kenneth Dr.
62 B1 St. Kilda Dr.
60 B2 St. Margarets Pl.
  Bridgegate
61 B4 St. Marnock St.

60 A1 St. Marys La.
  West Nile St.
65 A3 St. Monance St.
60 A2 St. Mungo Av.
60 A2 St. Mungo Pl.
60 B2 St. Ninian St.
60 A1 St. Peters La.
  Blythswood St.
64 C1 St. Peters St.
56 A1 St. Ronans Dr.
65 B3 St. Valleyfield St.
  Ayr St.
59 A3 St. Vincent Cres.
59 A4 St. Vincent Cres. La.
  Corunna St.
60 A1 St. Vincent La.
  Hope St.
60 A2 St. Vincent Pl.
59 A4 St. Vincent St.
59 A4 St. Vincent Ter.
58 B1 Salen St.
63 B3 Salisbury Pl.
  Great Western Rd.
60 C1 Salisbury St.
60 C1 Salkeld St.
64 B1 Salmona St.
60 B2 Saltmarket
60 B2 Saltmarket Pl.
  King St.
63 B3 Saltoun Gdns.
  Roxburgh St.
63 B3 Saltoun La.
  Ruthven St.
63 B3 Saltoun St.
63 B4 Sanda St.
63 A3 Sandbank Av.
63 A3 Sandbank Dr.
63 A3 Sandbank St.
62 C1 Sandeman St.
63 A4 Sandfield St.
  Maryhill Rd.
60 C2 Sandiefield La.
60 C2 Sandiefield Rd.
65 C4 Sandmill St.
63 B3 Sandringham La.
  Kersland St.
62 C2 Sandy Rd.
59 A4 Sandyford Pl.
  Sauciehall St.
63 C4 Sandyford Place La.
  Elderslie St.
59 A3 Sandyford St.
61 A4 Sannox Gdns.
64 A2 Saracen Gdns.
60 B2 Saracen Head La.
  Gallowgate
64 B2 Saracen St.
63 B3 Sardinia La.
  Great George St.
63 B3 Sardinia Ter.
  Cecil St.
59 A4 Sauchiehall St.
61 C3 Savoy Arcade
  Main St.
61 C3 Savoy St.
64 C1 Sawfield Pl.
  Garscube Rd.
62 C1 Sawmill Rd.
64 C1 Sawmillfield St.
61 C4 Scapa St.
  Springfield Rd.
60 B2 Schipka Pass.
  Gallowgate
64 B2 Scone St.
59 B4 Scotland St.
59 B3 Scotland St. W.
63 C3 Scotstoun Mill Rd.
  Patrick Bridge St.
64 C1 Scott St.
63 C4 Seamore St.
57 A4 Seath St.
59 B4 Seaward La.
  Seaward St.
59 B4 Seaward St.
57 C3 Second Av.
58 C2 Second Gdns.
62 A1 Selborne Pl.
  Selborne Rd.
62 A1 Selborne Place La.
  Selborne Rd.
62 A1 Selborne Rd.
61 A3 Seton Ter.
59 A4 Shaftsbury St.
  Argyle St.
59 A4 Shaftsbury St.
63 A4 Shakespeare St.
62 A1 Shamrock Cotts.
  Crow Rd.
64 C1 Shamrock St.
59 A3 Shandon St.
  Govan Rd.

63 A4	Shanks St.
63 A4	Shannon St.
58 A2	Sharp St.
59 B3	Sharrocks St.
	Clifford St.
58 A2	Shaw St.
56 B1	Shawbridge St.
56 B1	Shawhill Rd.
56 B2	Shawlands Arcade
56 B2	Shawlands Sq.
56 A1	Shawmoss Rd.
63 A4	Shawpark St.
59 B4	Shearer La.
59 B4	Shearer Pl.
62 A2	Shelley Ct.
	Shelley Rd.
62 A1	Shelley Rd.
65 B3	Sheppard St.
	Cowlairs Rd.
59 C3	Sherbrooke Av.
59 C3	Sherbrooke Dr.
59 B4	Shields Rd.
60 B2	Shipbank La.
	Clyde St.
63 A4	Shortbridge St.
	Shanks St.
63 A4	Shuna Pl.
63 A4	Shuna St.
60 A2	Shuttle La.
	George St.
60 A2	Shuttle St.
65 C4	Siemens Pl.
65 C4	Siemens St.
60 C2	Silverfir St.
61 B3	Silvergrove St.
63 B4	Simpson St.
56 B2	Sinclair Dr.
62 A1	Skaterig La.
62 A1	Skaterigg Rd.
	Crow Rd.
58 A2	Skene Rd.
58 A1	Skipness Dr.
56 B2	Skirving St.
61 B4	Slatefield St.
59 B4	Sleads St.
64 B2	Sloy St.
63 A4	Smeaton St.
62 C1	Smith St.
61 B4	Society St.
61 B4	Soho St.
63 C4	Somerset Pl.
63 C4	Somerset Place Meuse
	Elderslie St.
57 .B3	Somerville Dr.
61 C4	Sorn St.
57 A3	South Annandale St.
62 C1	South Cotts.
	Curle St.
60 A2	South Exchange Ct.
	Queen St.
60 A2	South Frederick St.
	Ingram St.
60 B1	South Portland St.
63 C4	South Woodside Rd.
62 A2	Southampton Dr.
62 A1	Southbrae La.
	Milner Rd.
58 A2	Southcroft St.
65 B3	Southlock St.
63 A3	Southmuir Pl.
63 C3	Southpark Av.
63 B4	Southpark La.
	Glasgow St.
63 C4	Southpark Ter.
	Southpark Av.
57 C4	Southwood Dr.
57 B3	Spean St.
65 B3	Spingburn Way
60 B2	Spoutmouth
60 C2	Spring La.
	Lawmoor St.
63 B4	Springbank St.
65 A3	Springburn Rd.
65 B3	Springburn Way
61 C4	Springfield Rd.
56 A2	Springhill Gdns.
59 C3	Springkell Av.
58 C2	Springkell Dr.
56 A1	Springkell Gate
65 B3	Springvale Ter.
	Hillkirk Pl.
64 A2	Spruce St.
62 C1	Squire St.
61 A4	Staffa St.
59 A3	Stag St.
63 B4	Stair St.
63 B4	Stamford St.
59 B4	Stanley St.
59 B4	Stanley Street La.
	Milnpark St.
57 B3	Stanmore Rd.

60 B2	Steel St.
61 B3	Stevenson St.
64 C1	Stewart St.
62 C2	Stewartville St.
60 B1	Stirling Fauld Pl.
60 A2	Stirling St.
63 A3	Stirrat St.
59 A4	Stobcross Rd.
61 B4	Stobo St.
60 B2	Stockwell Pl.
60 B2	Stockwell St.
63 A3	Stonefield Av.
64 B1	Stonyhurst St.
63 A4	Stratford St.
63 C3	Strathallan La.
	Highburgh Rd.
63 C3	Strathallan Ter.
	Caledon St.
63 A3	Strathcarron Pl.
	Gelnfinnan Rd.
62 A1	Strathcona St.
63 C4	Strathmore Gdns.
	Gibson St.
63 A3	Strathy Pl.
	Glenfinnan Rd.
56 B2	Strathyre St.
63 B4	Striven Gdns.
65 C4	Stroma St.
60 C1	Stromness St.
64 A1	Stronend St.
65 C4	Stronsay St.
57 C3	Struan Gdns.
57 C3	Struan Rd.
61 B3	Suffolk St.
	Kent St.
61 B3	Summer St.
62 C1	Summerfield Cotts.
	Smith St.
61 C4	Summerfield Pl.
	Ardenlea St.
58 A2	Summertown Rd.
58 B1	Sunart Rd.
61 C4	Sunnybank St.
64 B1	Sunnylaw St.
60 C1	Surrey La.
	Pollokshaws Rd.
59 B4	Sussex St.
59 C3	Sutherland Av.
64 C2	Swan La.
61 B3	Sword St.
62 B2	Sydenham La.
	Crown Rd. S.
63 B3	Sydenham Rd.
60 A1	Sydney Ct.
	Argyle St.
61 B3	Sydney St.
65 B3	Syriam Pl.
	Syriam St.
65 B3	Syriam St.
	T
63 A4	Tamshill St.
61 B4	Tamworth St.
	Rimsdale St.
57 C3	Tankerland Rd.
58 C1	Tanna Dr.
56 C2	Tannahill Rd.
64 B1	Tannock St.
56 B1	Tantallon Rd.
58 A2	Taransay St.
56 C1	Tarbolton Rd.
58 B1	Tarland St.
56 B1	Tassie St.
56 C1	Tavistock Dr.
60 A2	Taylor Pl.
60 A2	Taylor St.
61 B3	Templeton St.
56 A1	Terregles Av.,
56 A1	Terregles Cres.
56 A1	Terregles Dr.
59 A3	Teviot St.
63 B4	Teviot Ter.
	Sanda St.
65 C3	Tharsis St.
57 B3	Third Av.
58 C2	Third Gdns.
62 A1	Thistle Cotts.
	Crow Rd.
60 B2	Thistle St.
61 B4	Thomson St.
62 C2	Thorn St.
	Dumbarton Rd.
63 C3	Thornbank St.
	Yorkhill Parade
63 A3	Thornbridge Av.
	Balcarres Av.
56 A2	Thorncliffe Gdns.
59 C4	Thorncliffe La.
62 C2	Thornwood Av.
62 C1	Thornwood Dr.,

62 C2	Thornwood Gdns.
62 B2	Thornwood Pl.
62 C1	Thornwood Rd.
62 C1	Thornwood Ter.
59 A3	Three Ell Rd.
	Govan Rd.
63 C3	Thurso St.
	Dumbarton Rd.
62 B2	Tibbermore Rd.
63 B4	Tillie St.
56 C1	Tinto Rd.
56 A1	Titwood Rd.
61 B3	Tobago Pl.
61 B3	Tobago St.
59 B3	Toll La.
	Paisley Rd. W.
60 B2	Tontine La.
	Bell St.
58 B1	Torbreck St.
63 C3	Torness St.
64 B2	Torr St.
65 B3	Torrance St.
58 C2	Torridon Av.
56 A2	Torrisdale St.
57 A4	Toryglen St.
59 B4	Tower St.
65 B4	Towerhill Ter.
	Broomfield Rd.
61 A3	Townmill Rd.
64 C2	Townsend St.
56 B1	Tracy St.
60 B1	Tradeston St.
61 C3	Trafalgar St.
56 B1	Trefoil Av.
60 B2	Trongate
64 B1	Troon St.
62 B1	Tudor Rd.
64 B1	Trossachs St.
61 C3	Tullis Ct.
61 C3	Tullis St.
57 C3	Tulloch St.
59 A4	Tunnel St.
62 B2	Turnberry Av.
62 B2	Turnberry Rd.,
60 B2	Turnbull St.
60 C2	Turnlaw St.
60 C1	Turriff St.
64 C2	Tyndrum St.
	U
58 A1	Uist St.
58 B1	Ulva St.
56 B2	Underwood Rd.
	Tantallon Rd.
60 A1	Union Pl.
	Gordon St.
60 A1	Union St.
64 C1	Unity Pl.
	St. Peters St.
63 C3	University Av.
63 C3	University Gdns.
63 C3	University St.
60 A2	Ure Pl.
	Montrose St.
58 B2	Urrdale Rd.
	V
57 B3	Valeview Ter.
65 B3	Valleyfield St.
62 B1	Varna La.
62 B1	Varna Rd.
56 A2	Vennard Gdns.
64 B2	Vere St.
59 B4	Vermont St.
58 A2	Vicarfield Pl.
	Vicarfield St.
63 B3	Victoria Circus
63 B3	Victoria Cres.
	Dowanside Rd.
63 B3	Victoria Cres. La.
	Victoria Crescent Rd.
63 B3	Victoria Cres. Rd.
63 B3	Victoria Cross
	Victoria Rd.
62 B1	Victoria Park Dr. N.
62 B1	Victoria Park Gdns. N.
62 B1	Victoria Park Gdns. S.
57 A3	Viewfield Av.
63 C4	Viewfield La.,
	Gibson St.
63 C4	Viewfield Ter.
	Southpark Av.
61 A4	Viewpark Av.
65 A3	Viewpoint Pl.
65 A3	Viewpoint Rd.
61 B3	Villiers Ct.
	Sword St.
62 C2	Vine St.

61 B4	Vinegarhill St.
63 B3	Vinicombe La.
	Vinicombe St.
63 B3	Vinicombe St.
64 C2	Vintner St.
60 A2	Virginia Bldgs.
	Virginia St.
60 A2	Virginia Ct.
	Virginia St.
60 A2	Virginia Pl.
60 A2	Virginia St.
65 B3	Vulcan St.
	W
60 B2	Waddel Ct.
60 C2	Waddel St.
62 C2	Walker Ct.
	Walker St.
62 C2	Walker St.
61 C4	Walkinshaw St.
60 B1	Wallace St.
65 A4	Wallacewell Cres.
65 A4	Wallacewell Pl.
65 A4	Wallacewell Rd.
60 A2	Walls St.
59 B3	Walmer Cres.
59 B3	Walmer Ter.
	Paisley Rd. W.
64 A2	Walnut Cres.
64 A2	Walnut Pl.
64 A2	Walnut Rd.
56 B2	Walton St.
58 A2	Wanlock St.
65 A4	Wardhill Rd.
58 A2	Wardrop St.
59 A4	Warp La.
	Argyle St.
57 A3	Warren St.
59 A4	Warroch St.
60 A1	Washington St.
60 A1	Waterloo La.
	Waterloo St.
60 A1	Waterloo St.
60 C2	Waterside St.
60 B2	Watson St.,
59 B4	Watt St.
56 A2	Waverley Gdns.
56 A2	Waverley St.
61 B4	Waverley Ter.
	Whitevale St.
60 A2	Weaver St.
61 C4	Webster St.
56 B1	Well Grn.
61 B3	Well St.
60 C1	Wellcroft Pl.
65 B3	Wellfield St.
60 A1	Wellington La.
	West Campbell St.
60 A1	Wellington St.
61 A3	Wellpark St.
61 B3	Wellpark St.
60 A1	West Campbell La.
	West Campbell St.
60 A1	West George La.
	West Campbell St.
60 A1	West George St.
64 C1	West Graham St.
59 A4	West Greenhill Pl.
60 A1	West Nile St.
63 C4	West Princes St.
60 A1	West Regent La.
	Renfield St.
60 A1	West Regent St.
60 A1	West St.
60 C1	West St.
63 C4	Westbank La.
	Gibson St.
63 C4	Westbank Quad.
	Gibson St.
63 C4	Westbank Ter.
	Gibson St.
63 B3	Westbourne Gdns. La.
	Lorraine Rd.
63 B3	Westbourne Gdns. N.
63 B3	Westbourne Gdns. S.
63 B3	Westbourne Gdns. W.
62 B2	Westbourne Rd.
62 B2	Westbourne Ter. La.
	Westbourne Rd.
62 B1	Westbrae Dr.
56 A2	Westclyffe St.
63 C4	Westend Park St.
64 B1	Wester Common Dr.
64 B1	Wester Common Rd.
64 B1	Wester Common Ter.
61 A3	Westercraigs
64 B2	Westerhill St.
57 C3	Westknowe Gdns.
	Broomieknowe Rd.
63 B3	Westminster Gdns.
	Kersland St.

59 A4	Westminster Ter.
	Claremont St.
57 A3	Westmoreland St.
64 A2	Westray Circus
62 A2	Weymouth Dr.
56 A1	Whins Rd.
62 C2	White St.
59 B3	Whitefield Rd.
59 A4	Whitehall Ct.
59 A4	Whitehall St.
61 A4	Whitehill Gdns.
	Garthland Dr.
61 A4	Whitehill St.
61 B4	Whitevale St.
62 A1	Whittingehame Dr.
62 A2	Whittingehame Gdns
64 A1	Whitworth St.
58 A2	Wick St.
64 B1	Wigton St.
61 B4	Wilkie St.
59 A4	William St.
	Shaftsbury St.
62 A1	Willoughby Dr.
63 C4	Willowbank Cres.
63 C4	Willowbank St.
60 A2	Wilson St.
63 B4	Wilton Cres.
63 B4	Wilton Crescent La.
	Wilton Cres.
63 B4	Wilton Ct.
63 B4	Wilton Dr.
63 B4	Wilton Gdns.
63 B4	Wilton Mansions
	Wilton St.
63 B4	Wilton St.
62 A2	Winchester Dr.
56 C1	Windhill Pl.
	Windhill Rd.
56 C1	Windmill Pl.
	Windhill Rd.
60 B1	Windmillcroft Quay
64 C1	Windsor St.
64 C1	Windsor Ter.
63 A3	Winton Dr.
63 A3	Winton La.
61 A3	Wishart St.
60 C2	Wolseley St.
61 A4	Wood St.
56 C1	Woodburn Rd.
62 B1	Woodcroft Av.
62 B1	Woodcroft Ter.
	Crow Rd.
62 A1	Woodend Dr.
56 B2	Woodford St.
57 C4	Woodgreen Av.
65 A4	Woodhill Rd.
57 C4	Woodholm Av.
63 C4	Woodlands Dr.
63 C4	Woodlands Gate
63 C4	Woodlands Rd.
63 C4	Woodlands Ter.
57 C3	Woodlinn Av.
59 C3	Woodrow Circus
59 C3	Woodrow Pl.
	Maxwell Dr.
59 C3	Woodrow Rd.
63 C4	Woodside Cres.
63 C4	Woodside Place La.
	Elderslie St.
63 B4	Woodside Rd.
63 B4	Woodside Ter.
63 C4	Woodside Terrace La
	Woodlands Rd.
56 A1	Woodstock Av.
62 B2	Woodville St.
61 A3	Wright St.
63 A3	Wyndford Dr.
63 A3	Wyndford Pl.
	Wyndford Rd.
63 A3	Wyndford Rd.
63 B3	Wyndham St.
61 B4	Wyper Pl.
	Gallowgate
	Y
63 B4	Yarrow Gdns.
61 B4	Yate St.
60 A1	York La.
	York St.
60 B1	York St.
59 A3	Yorkhill La.
	Yorkhill St.
63 C3	Yorkhill Par.
59 A3	Yorkhill St.
65 B4	Young Ter.